2016

The official list of birds o

La lista oficial de las

Asociación Ornitológica de Costa Rica
Committee on Rare Species and Ornithological Registers in Costa Rica (Scientific Committee - AOCR)

AOCR
ASOCIACIÓN ORNITOLÓGICA DE COSTA RICA

The Costa Rican Ornithological Association's Committee on Rare Species and Ornithological Registers in Costa Rica - Asociación Ornitológica de Costa Rica (AOCR): Richard Garrigues, Marcela Araya-Salas, Pablo Camacho-Varela, Johel Chaves-Campos, Alejandra Martínez-Salinas, Michel Montoya, Gerardo Obando-Calderón, Oscar Ramírez-Alán
Cover photo, *Habia atrimaxillaris* by Susana García Blanco

Originally published in *Zeledonia* 19-2. Noviembre 2015. Boletín de la Asociación Ornitológica de Costa Rica. San José, Costa Rica.

ISBN-13: 978-1519361066
ISBN-10: 1519361068

La lista oficial de las aves de Costa Rica

Total de especies oficiales: 911

Estatus/Status:

SC	Sin comprobante (Fondo gris)	Without voucher (Gray background)
R	Residente	Resident
RR	Residente reproductivo	Breeding resident
R?	Residencia incierta	Residence uncertain
M	Migratorio	Migratory
M?	Migrant status uncertain	Migratory status uncertain
A	Accidental	Accidental
END	Especies endémicas para Costa Rica y la región	Endemic species for Costa Rica and the region

More information: http://listaoficialavesdecostarica.wordpress.com/

Forms for reporting sightings of rare birds or new species: http://listaoficialavesdecostarica.wordpress.com/reporte-y-procedimiento/

Taxonomy and English names updated to 2015 according to the Supplement 56 Chesser *et al. The Auk* 132(3) pp. 748-764. Julio 2015. By the American Ornithologists' Union (AOU).

#	Order-Family-Taxa	English name	Nombre en Español / (Común en Costa Rica)	Status			
	Tinamiformes						
	Tinamidae (5)						
1	*Nothocercus bonapartei*	Highland Tinamou	Tinamú Serrano (Gallina de monte de Altura, Gongolona)	R			
2	*Tinamus major*	Great Tinamou	Tinamú Grande (Gallina de monte, Perdiz, Gongolona, Yerre)	R			
3	*Crypturellus soui*	Little Tinamou	Tinamú Chico (Gallina de monte Chica, Gongolona, Yerre, Ponchita)	R			
4	*Crypturellus cinnamomeus*	Thicket Tinamou	Tinamú Canelo (Gallina de monte, Gongolona, Perdiz)	R			
5	*Crypturellus boucardi*	Slaty-breasted Tinamou	Tinamú Pizarroso (Gallina de monte Patirroja)	R			
	Anseriformes						
	Anatidae (21)						
6	*Dendrocygna viduata*	White-faced Whistling-Duck	Pijije Cariblanco (Piche Careto)	R?			
7	*Dendrocygna autumnalis*	Black-bellied Whistling-Duck	Pijije Común (Piche, Quichichi, Pichichi)	R			
8	*Dendrocygna bicolor*	Fulvous Whistling-Duck	Pijije Canelo (Piche Canelo)	R			
9	*Sarkidiornis melanotos*	Comb Duck	Pato Crestudo	A			
10	*Cairina moschata*	Muscovy Duck	Pato Real (Pato Perulero)	R			
11	*Anas americana*	American Wigeon	Pato Calvo (Carraco)	M			
12	*Anas platyrhynchos*	Mallard	Pato Cabeciverde (Carraco)	M			
13	*Anas discors*	Blue-winged Teal	Cerceta Aliazul (Pato Canadiense, Zarceta, Carraco)	M			
14	*Anas cyanoptera*	Cinnamon Teal	Cerceta Castaña (Carraco)	M			
15	*Anas clypeata*	Northern Shoveler	Pato Cuchara (Carraco)	M			
16	*Anas bahamensis*	White-cheeked Pintail	Pato Gargantilla	A			
17	*Anas acuta*	Northern Pintail	Pato Rabudo (Carraco Colilargo)	M			
18	*Anas crecca*	Green-winged Teal	Cerceta Aliverde (Carraco, Zarceta)	M			
19	*Aythya valisineria*	Canvasback	Porrón Picudo	A			

20	*Aythya americana*	Redhead	Porrón Americano (Pato Cabeza Roja)	A				
21	*Aythya collaris*	Ring-necked Duck	Porrón Collarejo (Pato)	M				
22	*Aythya marila*	Greater Scaup	Porrón Mayor (Pato)	A- SC				
23	*Aythya affinis*	Lesser Scaup	Porrón Menor (Pato)	M				
24	*Lophodytes cucullatus*	Hooded Merganser	Serreta Capuchona (Pato de Cresta)	A				
25	*Nomonyx dominicus*	Masked Duck	Pato Enmascarado	R				
26	*Oxyura jamaicensis*	Ruddy Duck	Pato Cariblanco	A				
	Galliformes							
	Cracidae (5)							
27	*Ortalis vetula*	Plain Chachalaca	Chachalaca Olivácea (Chachalaca)	R				
28	*Ortalis cinereiceps*	Gray-headed Chachalaca	Chachalaca Cabecigrís (Chachalaca, Pavita)	R				
29	*Penelope purpurascens*	Crested Guan	Pava Crestada (Pava Granadera)	R				
30	*Chamaepetes unicolor*	Black Guan	Pava Negra (Pajuila)	R-END				
31	*Crax rubra*	Great Curassow	Pavón Grande (Pavón, Granadera)	R				
	Odontophoridae (7)							
32	*Dendrortyx leucophrys*	Buffy-crowned Wood-Partridge	Perdiz Montañera (Chirrascuá)	R				
33	*Colinus cristatus*	Crested Bobwhite	Codorniz Crestada (Codorniz de Monte)	R				
34	*Odontophorus gujanensis*	Marbled Wood-Quail	Codorniz Carirroja o Corcovado (Julián Piojo)	R				
35	*Odontophorus melanotis*	Black-eared Wood-Quail	Codorniz Orejinegra (Chirrascuá, Gallinita)	R-END				
36	*Odontophorus leucolaemus*	Black-breasted Wood-Quail	Codorniz Pechinegra (Gallinita de Monte, Chirrascuá, Huevos de Chancho)	R-END				
37	*Odontophorus guttatus*	Spotted Wood-Quail	Codorniz Moteada o Pintada	R				
38	*Rhynchortyx cinctus*	Tawny-faced Quail	Codorniz Carirrufa	R				
	Podicipediformes							
	Podicipedidae (3)							
39	*Tachybaptus dominicus*	Least Grebe	Zambullidor Enano	R				

40	*Podilymbus podiceps*	Pied-billed Grebe	Zambullidor Piquipinto (Pico Pinto)	R, M?			
41	*Podiceps nigricollis*	Eared Grebe	Zambullidor Mediano	A- SC			
	Procellariiformes						
	Diomedeidae (1)						
42	*Phoebastria irrorata*	Waved Albatross	Albatros de Galápagos	A			
	Procellariidae (15)						
43	*Pterodroma hasitata*	Black-capped Petrel	Petrel Gorrinegro	A- SC			
44	*Pterodroma phaeopygia*	Galapagos Petrel	Petrel de Galápagos, Petrel Lomioscuro	A			
45	*Pterodroma rostrata*	Tahiti Petrel	Petrel de Tahiti	M			
46	*Procellaria parkinsoni*	Parkinson's Petrel	Petrel de Parkinson	M			
47	*Calonectris diomedea*	Cory's Shearwater	Pardela de Cory, Pardela Cenicienta	A			
48	*Puffinus creatopus*	Pink-footed Shearwater	Pardela Blanca Común	M			
49	*Pufinus gravis*	Great Shearwater	Pardela Mayor	A			
50	*Puffinus pacificus*	Wedge-tailed Shearwater	Pardela Colicuña	M			
51	*Puffinus griseus*	Sooty Shearwater	Pardela Sombría	M			
52	*Puffinus tenuirostris*	Short-tailed Shearwater	Pardela Colicorta	M?- SC			
53	*Puffinus nativitatis*	Christmas Shearwater	Pardela de Navidad, Pardela de Christmas	A			
54	*Puffinus subalaris*	Galapagos Shearwater	Pardela de las Galápagos	M			
55	*Puffinus puffinus*	Manx Shearwater	Pardela Manx	A- SC			
56	*Puffinus opisthomelas*	Black-vented Shearwater	Pardela Culinegra	A			
57	*Puffinus lherminieri*	Audubon's Shearwater	Pardela de Audubon	M			
	Hydrobatidae (8)						
58	*Oceanites oceanicus*	Wilson's Storm-Petrel	Paiño de Wilson	M- SC			
59	*Pelagodroma marina*	White-faced Storm-Petrel	Paiño Pechialbo	M- SC			
60	*Oceanodroma leucorhoa*	Leach's Storm-Petrel	Paiño de Leach	M			

61	*Oceanodroma castro*	Band-rumped Storm-Petrel	Paiño Rabifajeado	A- SC			
62	*Oceanodroma tethys*	Wedge-rumped Storm-Petrel	Paiño Danzarin	M			
63	*Oceanodroma melania*	Black Storm-Petrel	Paiño Negro	M			
64	*Oceanodroma markhami*	Markham's Storm-Petrel	Paiño de Markham	M			
65	*Oceanodroma microsoma*	Least Storm-Petrel	Paiño Menudo	M			
	Phaethontiformes						
	Phaethontidae (3)						
66	*Phaethon lepturus*	White-tailed Tropicbird	Rabijunco Cola Blanca	A			
67	*Phaethon aethereus*	Red-billed Tropicbird	Rabijunco Piquirrojo	M			
68	*Phaethon rubricauda*	Red-tailed Tropicbird	Rabijunco Cola Roja	A			
	Ciconiiformes						
	Ciconiidae (3)						
69	*Ciconia maguari*	Maguari Stork	Cigüeña Maguari	A			
70	*Jabiru mycteria*	Jabiru	Jabirú (Galán Sin Ventura, Veterano)	R			
71	*Mycteria americana*	Wood Stork	Cigüeñón (Garzón, Guairón, Cigüeña)	R, M			
	Suliformes						
	Fregatidae (2)						
72	*Fregata magnificens*	Magnificent Frigatebird	Rabihorcado Magno (Tijereta, Fragata, Zopilote de Mar)	R			
73	*Fregata minor*	Great Frigatebird	Rabihorcado Grande (Tijereta)	R			
	Sulidae (6)						
74	*Sula dactylatra*	Masked Booby	Piquero Blanco	R			
75	*Sula granti*	Nazca Booby	Piquero de Nazca	R?			
76	*Sula nebouxii*	Blue-footed Booby	Piquero Patiazul	M			
77	*Sula variegta*	Peruvian Booby	Piquero Peruano	A			
78	*Sula leucogaster*	Brown Booby	Piquero Moreno (Monjita, Alcatraz)	R			

79	*Sula sula*	Red-footed Booby	Piquero Patirrojo	R			
	Phalacrocoracidae (1)						
80	*Phalacrocorax brasilianus*	Neotropic Cormorant	Cormorán Neotropical (Pato Chancho, Pato de Agua, Bigua)	R			
	Anhingidae (1)						
81	*Anhinga anhinga*	Anhinga	Aninga (Pato Aguja)	R			
	Pelecaniformes						
	Pelecanidae (2)						
82	*Pelecanus erythrorhynchos*	American White Pelican	Pelícano Blanco Americano	A			
83	*Pelecanus occidentalis*	Brown Pelican	Pelícano Pardo (Buchón, Pelícano, Alcatraz)	R			
	Ardeidae (19)						
84	*Botaurus pinnatus*	Pinnated Bittern	Avetoro Neotropical (Puncus, Mirasol)	R			
85	*Botaurus lentiginosus*	American Bittern	Avetoro Norteño (Puncus)	M?			
86	*Ixobrychus exilis*	Least Bittern	Avetorillo Pantanero (Mirasol)	R, M?			
87	*Tigrisoma lineatum*	Rufescent Tiger-Heron	Garza-Tigre de Selva (Martín Peña, Pájaro Vaco)	R			
88	*Tigrisoma fasciatum*	Fasciated Tiger-Heron	Garza-Tigre de Río (Martín Peña, Pájaro Vaco)	R			
89	*Tigrisoma mexicanum*	Bare-throated Tiger-Heron	Garza-Tigre Cuellinuda (Garzón, Martín Peña, Pájaro Vaco)	R			
90	*Ardea herodias*	Great Blue Heron	Garzón Azulado (Garza Ceniza, Garzón)	M			
91	*Ardea alba*	Great Egret	Garceta Grande (Garza Real)	R, M			
92	*Egretta thula*	Snowy Egret	Garceta Nivosa	R, M			
93	*Egretta caerulea*	Little Blue Heron	Garceta Azul (Garza Negra)	R, M			
94	*Egretta tricolor*	Tricolored Heron	Garceta Tricolor	R, M			
95	*Egretta rufescens*	Reddish Egret	Garceta Rojiza	M			
96	*Bubulcus ibis*	Cattle Egret	Garcilla Bueyera (Garcilla Ganadera, Garza Vaquera, Garza de Ganado)	R, M			
97	*Butorides virescens*	Green Heron	Garcilla Verde (Martín Peña)	R, M			
98	*Butorides striata*	Striated Heron	Garcilla Cuelligrís (Chocuaco, Martín Peña)	A			
99	*Agamia agami*	Agami Heron	Garza Pechicastaña (Agamia)	R			

100	*Nycticorax nycticorax*	Black-crowned Night-Heron	Martinete Coroninegro (Chocuaca)	R, M			
101	*Nyctanassa violacea*	Yellow-crowned Night-Heron	Martinete Cabecipinto	R, M			
102	*Cochlearius cochlearius*	Boat-billed Heron	Pico Cuchara (Chocuaco, Cuaca)	R			
	Threskiornithidae (5)						
103	*Eudocimus albus*	White Ibis	Ibis Blanco (Coco)	R			
104	*Plegadis falcinellus*	Glossy Ibis	Ibis Morito (Coco Negro)	R			
105	*Plegadis chihi*	White-faced Ibis	Ibis Cariblanco	M?			
106	*Mesembrinibis cayennensis*	Green Ibis	Ibis Verde (Coco Negro)	R			
107	*Platalea ajaja*	Roseate Spoonbill	Espátula Rosada (Garza Morena o Rosada, Pato Cuchara o Rosado)	R			
	Accipitriformes						
	Cathartidae (4)						
108	*Coragyps atratus*	Black Vulture	Zopilote Negro (Zoncho, Gallinazo)	R			
109	*Cathartes aura*	Turkey Vulture	Zopilote Cabecirrojo (Zonchite, Noneca)	R, M			
110	*Cathartes burrovianus*	Lesser Yellow-headed Vulture	Zopilote Cabecigualdo (Noneca)	R			
111	*Sarcoramphus papa*	King Vulture	Zopilote Rey (Rey Gallinazo, Rey de Zopilotes)	R			
	Pandionidae (1)						
112	*Pandion haliaetus*	Osprey	Águila Pescadora (Gavilán Pescador)	M			
	Accipitridae (39)						
113	*Leptodon cayanensis*	Gray-headed Kite	Gavilán Cabecigrís	R			
114	*Chondrohierax uncinatus*	Hook-billed Kite	Gavilán Piquiganchudo	R			
115	*Elanoides forficatus*	Swallow-tailed Kite	Elanio Tijereta (Gavilán Tijereta)	R, RR, M			
116	*Gampsonyx swainsonii*	Pearl Kite	Elanio Enano	R			
117	*Elanus leucurus*	White-tailed Kite	Elanio Coliblanco (Gavilán Bailarín, Gavilancillo Blanco)	R			
118	*Rostrhamus sociabilis*	Snail Kite	Elanio Caracolero (Gavilán Caracolero)	R			

119	*Harpagus bidentatus*	Double-toothed Kite	Gavilán Gorgirrayado	R				
120	*Ictinia mississippiensis*	Mississippi Kite	Elanio Colinegro	M				
121	*Ictinia plumbea*	Plumbeous Kite	Elanio Plomizo	RR, M				
122	*Busarellus nigricollis*	Black-collared Hawk	Gavilán de Ciénega (Gavilán Pescador)	R				
123	*Circus cyaneus*	Northern Harrier	Aguilucho Norteño	M				
124	*Accipiter poliogaster*	Gray-bellied Hawk	Gavilán Vientrigris	R?				
125	*Accipiter superciliosus*	Tiny Hawk	Gavilán Enano (Camaleón)	R				
126	*Accipiter striatus*	Sharp-shinned Hawk	Gavilán Pajarero (Camaleón)	M				
127	*Accipiter cooperii*	Cooper's Hawk	Gavilán de Cooper (Camaleón)	M				
128	*Accipiter bicolor*	Bicolored Hawk	Gavilán Bicolor (Camaleón)	R				
129	*Geranospiza caerulescens*	Crane Hawk	Gavilán Ranero (Caracolero)	R				
130	*Buteogallus anthracinus*	Common Black Hawk	Gavilán Cangrejero	R				
131	*Buteogallus meridionalis*	Savanna Hawk	Gavilán Sabanero	R?				
132	*Buteogallus urubitinga*	Great Black Hawk	Gavilán Negro Mayor (Aguilucho, Gavilán Silbero, Cangrejero)	R				
133	*Buteogallus solitarius*	Solitary Eagle	Águila Solitaria	R- SC				
134	*Morphnarchus princeps*	Barred Hawk	Gavilán Pechinegro	R				
135	*Rupornis magnirostris*	Roadside Hawk	Gavilán Chapulinero (Pata Podrida)	R				
136	*Parabuteo unicinctus*	Harris's Hawk	Gavilán Alicastaño	R, M?				
137	*Geranoaetus albicaudatus*	White-tailed Hawk	Gavilán Coliblanco (Gavilán Sabanero)	R				
138	*Pseudastur albicollis*	White Hawk	Gavilán Blanco	R				
139	*Leucopternis semiplumbeus*	Semiplumbeous Hawk	Gavilán Dorsiplomizo	R				
140	*Buteo plagiatus*	Gray Hawk	Gavilán Gris (Gavilán Pollero)	R				
141	*Buteo nitidus*	Gray-lined Hawk	Gavilán Gris Rayado (Gavilán Pollero)	R				
142	*Buteo platypterus*	Broad-winged Hawk	Gavilán Aludo (Gavilán Pollero)	M				
143	*Buteo brachyurus*	Short-tailed Hawk	Gavilán Colicorto	R, M				
144	*Buteo swainsoni*	Swainson's Hawk	Gavilán de Swainson	M				

145	*Buteo albonotatus*	Zone-tailed Hawk	Gavilán Colifajeado	R, M			
146	*Buteo jamaicensis*	Red-tailed Hawk	Gavilán Colirrojo (Gavilán Valdivia)	R, M			
147	*Morphnus guianensis*	Crested Eagle	Águila Crestada	R			
148	*Harpia harpyja*	Harpy Eagle	Águila Arpía (Aguilucho)	R			
149	*Spizaetus tyrannus*	Black Hawk-Eagle	Aguilillo Negro (Aguilucho)	R			
150	*Spizaetus ornatus*	Ornate Hawk-Eagle	Aguilillo Penachudo (Aguilucho)	R			
151	*Spizaetus melanoleucus*	Black-and-white Hawk-Eagle	Aguilillo Blanco y Negro (Águila Marcial)	R			
	Eurypygiformes						
	Eurypygidae (1)						
152	*Eurypyga helias*	Sunbittern	Garza del Sol (Sol y Luna, Ave Canasta)	R			
	Gruiformes						
	Rallidae (16)						
153	*Micropygia schomburgkii*	Ocellated Crake	Polluela Ocelada	R			
154	*Laterallus ruber*	Ruddy Crake	Polluela Colorada	R?- SC			
155	*Laterallus albigularis*	White-throated Crake	Polluela Gargantiblanca (Freidora, Huevo frito)	R			
156	*Laterallus exilis*	Gray-breasted Crake	Polluela Pechigrís	R			
157	*Laterallus jamaicensis*	Black Rail	Polluela Negra	R?, M?- SC			
158	*Rallus crepitans*	Clapper Rail	Rascón Picudo	R?, M?			
159	*Aramides axillaris*	Rufous-necked Wood-Rail	Rascón Cuellirrufo	R			
160	*Aramides cajaneus*	Gray-necked Wood-Rail	Rascón Cuelligrís (Chirincoco, Pomponé, Pone-pone)	R			
161	*Amaurolimnas concolor*	Uniform Crake	Rascón Café	R			
162	*Porzana carolina*	Sora	Polluela Sora o Norteña	M			
163	*Porzana flaviventer*	Yellow-breasted Crake	Polluela Pechiamarilla	R			
164	*Neocrex erythrops*	Paint-billed Crake	Polluela Piquirroja	R			
165	*Pardirallus maculatus*	Spotted Rail	Rascón Moteado	R			

166	*Porphyrio martinicus*	Purple Gallinule	Gallareta Morada (Polla de Agua, Gallina de Agua, Calamón Morada)	R				
167	*Gallinula galeata*	Common Gallinule	Gallareta Frentirroja (Gallineta)	R, M?				
168	*Fulica americana*	American Coot	Focha Americana	R, M				
	Heliornithidae (1)							
169	*Heliornis fulica*	Sungrebe	Pato Cantil (Perrito de Agua, Toboba)	R				
	Aramidae (1)							
170	*Aramus guarauna*	Limpkin	Carao (Correa)	R				
	Charadriiformes							
	Burhinidae (1)							
171	*Burhinus bistriatus*	Double-striped Thick-Knee	Alcaraván Americano (Alcaraván)	R				
	Recurvirostridae (2)							
172	*Himantopus mexicanus*	Black-necked Stilt	Cigüeñuela Cuellinegro (Soldadito)	R, M				
173	*Recurvirostra americana*	American Avocet	Avoceta Americana	M				
	Haematopodidae (1)							
174	*Haematopus palliatus*	American Oystercatcher	Ostrero Americano	R, M				
	Charadriidae (10)							
175	*Vanellus chilensis*	Southern Lapwing	Chorlitazo Sureño	R				
176	*Pluvialis squatarola*	Black-bellied Plover	Chorlito Gris (Avefría)	M				
177	*Pluvialis dominica*	American Golden-Plover	Chorlito Dorado Menor	M				
178	*Pluvialis fulva*	Pacific Golden-Plover	Chorlito Dorado del Pacífico	A				
179	*Charadrius collaris*	Collared Plover	Chorlitejo Collarejo (Turillo)	R				
180	*Charadrius nivosus*	Snowy Plover	Chorlitejo Blanco o Patinegro (Chorlito, Turillo)	M				
181	*Charadrius wilsonia*	Wilson's Plover	Chorlitejo Picudo (Chorlito Gritón, Turillo)	R, M				
182	*Charadrius semipalmatus*	Semipalmated Plover	Chorlitejo Semipalmado (Chorlito, Turillo)	M				
183	*Charadrius melodus*	Piping Plover	Chorlitejo Silbador	A				

184	*Charadrius vociferus*	Killdeer	Chorlitejo Tildío o de Dos Collares (Pijije, Tildío)	R, M			
	Jacanidae (2)						
185	*Jacana spinosa*	Northern Jacana	Jacana Centroamericana (Cirujano, Gallito de Agua, Mulita, Yegüita)	R			
186	*Jacana jacana*	Wattled Jacana	Jacana Sureña	A			
	Scolopacidae (32)						
187	*Actitis macularius*	Spotted Sandpiper	Andarríos Maculado (Alzacolita, Piririza, Tigüiza)	M			
188	*Tringa solitaria*	Solitary Sandpiper	Andarríos Solitario (Tigüiza)	M			
189	*Tringa incana*	Wandering Tattler	Correlimos Vagabundo	M			
190	*Tringa melanoleuca*	Greater Yellowlegs	Patiamarillo Mayor (Correlimos Grande, Pijije, Zarceta)	M			
191	*Tringa semipalmata*	Willet	Pigüilo	M			
192	*Tringa flavipes*	Lesser Yellowlegs	Patiamarillo Menor (Pijije, Zarceta)	M			
193	*Bartramia longicauda*	Upland Sandpiper	Pradero (Gansa)	M			
194	*Numenius phaeopus*	Whimbrel	Zarapito Trinador (Cherelá, Zarceta)	M			
195	*Numenius americanus*	Long-billed Curlew	Zarapito Piquilargo	M			
196	*Limosa haemastica*	Hudsonian Godwit	Aguja Lomiblanca	M- SC			
197	*Limosa fedoa*	Marbled Godwit	Aguja Canela	M			
198	*Arenaria interpres*	Ruddy Turnstone	Vuelvepiedras Rojizo	M			
199	*Calidris canutus*	Red Knot	Correlimos Grande	M			
200	*Calidris virgata*	Surfbird	Chorlito de Rompientes	M			
201	*Calidris pugnax*	Ruff	Combatiente	M- SC			
202	*Calidris himantopus*	Stilt Sandpiper	Correlimos Patilargo (Patudo, Becacina)	M			
203	*Calidris ferruginea*	Curlew Sandpiper	Correlimos Zarapitín	M			
204	*Calidris alba*	Sanderling	Playero Arenero	M			
205	*Calidris alpina*	Dunlin	Correlimos Pechinegro	M			
206	*Calidris bairdii*	Baird's Sandpiper	Correlimos de Baird (Patudo, Becacina)	M			
207	*Calidris minutilla*	Least Sandpiper	Correlimos Menudo (Patudo, Becacina)	M			
208	*Calidris fuscicollis*	White-rumped Sandpiper	Correlimos Lomiblanco (Patudo, Becacina)	M			

209	*Calidris subruficollis*	Buff-breasted Sandpiper	Praderito Pechianteado (Zarceta)	M			
210	*Calidris melanotos*	Pectoral Sandpiper	Correlimos Pechirrayado (Patudo, Becacina)	M			
211	*Calidris pusilla*	Semipalmated Sandpiper	Correlimos Semipalmado	M			
212	*Calidris mauri*	Western Sandpiper	Correlimos Occidental (Patudo, Becacina)	M			
213	*Limnodromus griseus*	Short-billed Dowitcher	Agujeta Común	M			
214	*Limnodromus scolopaceus*	Long-billed Dowitcher	Agujeta Silbona	M			
215	*Gallinago delicata*	Wilson's Snipe	Becacina Común (Becada)	M			
216	*Phalaropus tricolor*	Wilson's Phalarope	Falaropo Tricolor	M			
217	*Phalaropus lobatus*	Red-necked Phalarope	Falaropo Picofino	M			
218	*Phalaropus fulicarius*	Red Phalarope	Falaropo Rojo	M			
	Stercorariidae (4)						
219	*Stercorarius maccormicki*	South Polar Skua	Salteador Polar	A- SC			
220	*Stercorarius pomarinus*	Pomarine Jaeger	Págalo Pomarino	M			
221	*Stercorarius parasiticus*	Parasitic Jaeger	Págalo Parásito	M			
222	*Stercorarius longicaudus*	Long-tailed Jaeger	Págalo Colilargo	A			
	Laridae (32)						
223	*Creagrus furcatus*	Swallow-tailed Gull	Gaviota Tijereta	M			
224	*Rissa tridactyla*	Black-legged Kittiwake	Gaviota Tridáctila, Gaviota Patinegra AOCR	A			
225	*Xema sabini*	Sabine's Gull	Gaviota de Sabine	M			
226	*Chroicocephalus philadelphia*	Bonaparte's Gull	Gaviota de Bonaparte	A			
227	*Chroicocephalus cirrocephalus*	Gray-hooded Gull	Gaviota Cabecigris	A			
228	*Leucophaeus modestus*	Gray Gull	Gaviota Torero, Garuma	A			
229	*Leucophaeus atricilla*	Laughing Gull	Gaviota Reidora	M			
230	*Leucophaeus pipixcan*	Franklin's Gull	Gaviota de Franklin	M			
231	*Larus heermanni*	Heermann's Gull	Gaviota de Heermann	A- SC			
232	*Larus delawarensis*	Ring-billed Gull	Gaviota Piquianillada	M			
233	*Larus occidentalis*	Western Gull	Gaviota Occidental	A			

234	*Larus californicus*	California Gull	Gaviota Californiana	A			
235	*Larus argentatus*	Herring Gull	Gaviota Argéntea	M			
236	*Larus dominicanus*	Kelp Gull	Gaviota Cocinera, Gaviota Dominicana	A			
237	*Anous stolidus*	Brown Noddy	Tiñosa Común (Charrán Negro)	R			
238	*Anous minutus*	Black Noddy	Tiñosa Negra (Charrán Negro Pequeño)	R			
239	*Gygis alba*	White Tern	Charrán Blanco (Palomita del Espíritu Santo)	R			
240	*Onychoprion fuscatus*	Sooty Tern	Charrán Sombrío	M			
241	*Onychoprion anaethetus*	Bridled Tern	Charrán Embridado	RR, M			
242	*Sternula antillarum*	Least Tern	Charrán Chico o Menudo	M			
243	*Phaetusa simplex*	Large-billed Tern	Charrán Picudo (Charrán de Río) AOCR	A			
244	*Gelochelidon nilotica*	Gull-billed Tern	Charrán Piquinegro	M			
245	*Hydroprogne caspia*	Caspian Tern	Pagaza Mayor o Piquirojo	M			
246	*Larosterna inca*	Inca Tern	Charrán Inca	A			
247	*Chlidonias niger*	Black Tern	Charrancito Negro o Fumarel	M			
248	*Sterna hirundo*	Common Tern	Charrán Común	M			
249	*Sterna paradisaea*	Arctic Tern	Charrán Viajero	M?- SC			
250	*Sterna forsteri*	Forster's Tern	Charrán de Forster	M			
251	*Thalasseus maximus*	Royal Tern	Pagaza Real	M			
252	*Thalasseus sandvicensis*	Sandwich Tern	Pagaza Puntiamarilla	M			
253	*Thalasseus elegans*	Elegant Tern	Pagaza Elegante	M			
254	*Rynchops niger*	Black Skimmer	Rayador Negro	M			
	Columbiformes						
	Columbidae (25)						
255	*Columba livia*	Rock Pigeon	Paloma Doméstica (Paloma de Castilla)	R			
256	*Patagioenas cayennensis*	Pale-vented Pigeon	Paloma Colorada (Paloma Morada)	R			
257	*Patagioenas speciosa*	Scaled Pigeon	Paloma Escamosa (Paloma Morada)	R			
258	*Patagioenas leucocephala*	White-crowned Pigeon	Paloma Coroniblanca	A			

259	*Patagioenas flavirostris*	Red-billed Pigeon	Paloma Piquirroja (Paloma Morada Común)	R				
260	*Patagioenas fasciata*	Band-tailed Pigeon	Paloma Collareja	R				
261	*Patagioenas subvinacea*	Ruddy Pigeon	Paloma Rojiza (Paloma Morada)	R				
262	*Patagioenas nigrirostris*	Short-billed Pigeon	Paloma Piquicorta (Paloma Morada, Dos-tontos-son)	R				
263	*Columbina inca*	Inca Dove	Tortolita Colilarga (San Juan, Tórtola)	R				
264	*Columbina passerina*	Common Ground-Dove	Tortolita Común (Tortolita, Palomita)	R				
265	*Columbina minuta*	Plain-breasted Ground-Dove	Tortolita Menuda (Tortolita, Conchita)	R				
266	*Columbina talpacoti*	Ruddy Ground-Dove	Tortolita Rojiza (Tortolita, Palomita Colorada)	R				
267	*Claravis pretiosa*	Blue Ground-Dove	Tortolita Azulada	R				
268	*Claravis mondetoura*	Maroon-chested Ground-Dove	Tortolita Serranera	R				
269	*Geotrygon montana*	Ruddy Quail-Dove	Paloma-Perdiz Rojiza	R				
270	*Geotrygon violacea*	Violaceous Quail-Dove	Paloma-Perdiz Violácea	R				
271	*Leptotrygon veraguensis*	Olive-backed Quail-Dove	Paloma-Perdiz Bigotiblanca	R				
272	*Leptotila verreauxi*	White-tipped Dove	Paloma Coliblanca (Coliblanca, Yuré)	R				
273	*Leptotila cassinii*	Gray-chested Dove	Paloma Pechigrís (Yuré)	R				
274	*Leptotila plumbeiceps*	Gray-headed Dove	Paloma Coronigrís (Yuré)	R				
275	*Zentrygon costaricensis*	Buff-fronted Quail-Dove	Paloma-Perdiz Costarriqueña	R-END				
276	*Zentrygon lawrencii*	Purplish-backed Quail-Dove	Paloma-Perdiz Sombría	R				
277	*Zentrygon chiriquensis*	Chiriqui Quail-Dove	Paloma-Perdiz Pechicanela	R-END				
278	*Zenaida asiatica*	White-winged Dove	Paloma Aliblanca (Arrocera)	R, M				
279	*Zenaida macroura*	Mourning Dove	Paloma Rabuda	R, M				
	Cuculiformes							
	Cuculidae (12)							
280	*Piaya cayana*	Squirrel Cuckoo	Cuco Ardilla (Bobo Chiso, Cacao, San Miguel)	R				

281	*Coccyzus americanus*	Yellow-billed Cuckoo	Cuclillo Piquigualdo	M				
282	*Coccyzus minor*	Mangrove Cuckoo	Cuclillo de Antifaz u Orejinegro	R?, M				
283	*Coccyzus ferrugineus*	Cocos Cuckoo	Cuclillo de la Isla del Coco	R-END				
284	*Coccyzus erythropthalmus*	Black-billed Cuckoo	Cuclillo Piquinegro	M				
285	*Tapera naevia*	Striped Cuckoo	Cuclillo Listado (Rondero, Tres Pesos, Ave de las Ánimas)	R				
286	*Dromococcyx phasianellus*	Pheasant Cuckoo	Cuclillo Faisán	R				
287	*Morococcyx erythropygus*	Lesser Ground-Cuckoo	Cuclillo Sabanero (Horero)	R				
288	*Neomorphus geoffroyi*	Rufous-vented Ground-Cuckoo	Cuco Hormiguero	R				
289	*Crotophaga major*	Greater Ani	Garrapatero Mayor (Tijo) AOCR	A				
290	*Crotophaga ani*	Smooth-billed Ani	Garrapatero Piquiliso (Tijo, Tinco)	R				
291	*Crotophaga sulcirostris*	Groove-billed Ani	Garrapatero Piquiestriado (Tijo, Tinco, Zopilotillo)	R				
	Strigiformes							
	Tytonidae (1)							
292	*Tyto alba*	Barn-Owl	Lechuza Ratonera (Lechuza de Campanario, Cara de Gato, Búho)	R				
	Strigidae (16)							
293	*Megascops cooperi*	Pacific Screech-Owl	Lechucita Sabanera (Ju de León, Estucurú o Sorococa)	R				
294	*Megascops choliba*	Tropical Screech-Owl	Lechucita Neotropical (Estucurú o Sorococa)	R				
295	*Megascops guatemalae*	Vermiculated Screech-Owl	Lechucita Vermiculada (Estucurú o Sorococa)	R				
296	*Megascops clarkii*	Bare-shanked Screech-Owl	Lechucita Serranera (Estucurú o Sorococa)	R-END				
297	*Lophostrix cristata*	Crested Owl	Búho Penachudo	R				
298	*Pulsatrix perspicillata*	Spectacled Owl	Búho de Anteojos (Oropopo)	R				
299	*Bubo virginianus*	Great Horned Owl	Búho Grande	R?				
300	*Glaucidium costaricanum*	Costa Rican Pygmy-Owl	Mochuelo Montañero	R-END				

301	*Glaucidium griseiceps*	Central American Pygmy-Owl	Mochuelo Enano	R				
302	*Glaucidium brasilianum*	Ferruginous Pygmy-Owl	Mochuelo Común (Cuatro Ojos, Majafierro)	R				
303	*Athene cunicularia*	Burrowing Owl	Lechuza Terrestre o Llanera	A				
304	*Ciccaba virgata*	Mottled Owl	Lechuza Café (Ju de León)	R				
305	*Ciccaba nigrolineata*	Black-and-white Owl	Lechuza Blanco y Negro	R				
306	*Asio flammeus*	Short-eared Owl	Lechuza Campestre	A				
307	*Pseudoscops clamator*	Striped Owl	Búho Listado	R				
308	*Aegolius ridgwayi*	Unspotted Saw-whet Owl	Lechucita Parda (Lechucita de Alfaro)	R				
	Caprimulgiformes							
	Caprimulgidae (10)							
309	*Lurocalis semitorquatus*	Short-tailed Nighthawk	Añapero Colicorto	R				
310	*Chordeiles acutipennis*	Lesser Nighthawk	Añapero Menor (Gavilán)	R, M				
311	*Chordeiles minor*	Common Nighthawk	Añapero Zumbón	RR, M				
312	*Nyctidromus albicollis*	Common Pauraque	Tapacaminos Común (Cuyeo, Pucuyo)	R				
313	*Nyctiphrynus ocellatus*	Ocellated Poorwill	Chotacabras Ocelado	R				
314	*Antrostomus carolinensis*	Chuck-will's-widow	Chotacabras de Paso	M				
315	*Antrostomus rufus*	Rufous Nightjar	Chotacabras Rojizo	R				
316	*Antrostomus vociferus*	Eastern Whip-poor-will	Chotacabras Norteño	M?				
317	*Antrostomus saturatus*	Dusky Nightjar	Chotacabras Sombrío (Tres Cobijas)	R-END				
318	*Hydropsalis cayennensis*	White-tailed Nightjar	Chotacabras Coliblanco	R				
	Nyctibiidae (3)							
319	*Nyctibius grandis*	Great Potoo	Nictibio Grande (Pájaro Estaca, Leona, Bruja)	R				
320	*Nyctibius griseus*	Common Potoo	Nictibio Común (Pájaro Estaca, Pájaro Palo)	R				
321	*Nyctibius jamaicensis*	Northern Potoo	Nictibio Norteño (Pájaro Estaca, Gozona) AOCR	R				
	Steatornithidae (1)							

322	*Steatornis caripensis*	Oilbird	Guácharo	R?			
	Apodiformes						
	Apodidae (11)						
323	*Cypseloides niger*	Black Swift	Vencejo Negro	R, M			
324	*Cypseloides cryptus*	White-chinned Swift	Vencejo Sombrío	R			
325	*Cypseloides cherriei*	Spot-fronted Swift	Vencejo de Cherrie	R			
326	*Streptoprocne rutila*	Chestnut-collared Swift	Vencejo Cuellicastaño	R			
327	*Streptoprocne zonaris*	White-collared Swift	Vencejón Collarejo (Golondrón)	R			
328	*Chaetura pelagica*	Chimney Swift	Vencejo de Paso	M			
329	*Chaetura vauxi*	Vaux's Swift	Vencejo Común	R			
330	*Chaetura fumosa*	Costa Rican Swift	Vencejo de Rabadilla Clara	R-END			
331	*Chaetura cinereiventris*	Gray-rumped Swift	Vencejo Lomigrís	R			
332	*Panyptila cayennensis*	Lesser Swallow-tailed Swift	Vencejo Tijereta Menor (Macuá)	R			
333	*Panyptila sanctihieronymi*	Great Swallow-tailed Swift	Vencejo Tijereta Mayor	A- SC			
	Trochilidae (52)						
334	*Florisuga mellivora*	White-necked Jacobin	Jacobino Nuquiblanco	R			
335	*Eutoxeres aquila*	White-tipped Sicklebill	Pico de Hoz	R			
336	*Glaucis aeneus*	Bronzy Hermit	Ermitaño Bronceado	R			
337	*Threnetes ruckeri*	Band-tailed Barbthroat	Ermitaño Barbudo	R			
338	*Phaethornis guy*	Green Hermit	Ermitaño Verde	R			
339	*Phaethornis longirostris*	Long-billed Hermit	Ermitaño Colilargo	R			
340	*Phaethornis striigularis*	Stripe-throated Hermit	Ermitaño Enano	R			
341	*Doryfera ludovicae*	Green-fronted Lancebill	Pico de Lanza Frentiverde	R			
342	*Colibri delphinae*	Brown Violetear	Colibrí Orejivioláceo Pardo	R			
343	*Colibri thalassinus*	Green Violetear	Colibrí Orejivioláceo Verde	R			
344	*Heliothryx barroti*	Purple-crowned Fairy	Colibrí Picopunzón	R			

345	*Anthracothorax prevostii*	Green-breasted Mango	Colibrí Manguito Pechiverde	R			
346	*Anthracothorax veraguensis*	Veraguan Mango	Colibrí Manguito de Veragua	R?			
347	*Discosura conversii*	Green Thorntail	Colibrí Colicerda Verde	R			
348	*Lophornis delattrei*	Rufous-crested Coquette	Coqueta Crestirrojiza	R?			
349	*Lophornis helenae*	Black-crested Coquette	Coqueta Crestinegra	R			
350	*Lophornis adorabilis*	White-crested Coquette	Coqueta Crestiblanca	R-END			
351	*Heliodoxa jacula*	Green-crowned Brilliant	Colibrí Brillante Frentiverde	R			
352	*Eugenes fulgens*	Magnificent Hummingbird	Colibrí Magnífico	R			
353	*Panterpe insignis*	Fiery-throated Hummingbird	Colibrí Garganta de Fuego	R-END			
354	*Heliomaster longirostris*	Long-billed Starthroat	Colibrí Piquilargo (Pochotero del Sur)	R			
355	*Heliomaster constantii*	Plain-capped Starthroat	Colibrí Pochotero	R			
356	*Lampornis hemileucus*	White-bellied Mountain-gem	Colibrí Montañes Vientriblanco	R-END			
357	*Lampornis calolaemus*	Purple-throated Mountain-gem	Colibrí Montañes Gorgimorado	R-END			
358	*Lampornis castaneoventris*	White-throated Mountain-gem	Colibrí Montañes Coligrís, Colibrí Montañes Gorgiblanco	R-END			
359	*Calliphlox bryantae*	Magenta-throated Woodstar	Colibrí Estrellita Gorgimorada	R-END			
360	*Archilochus colubris*	Ruby-throated Hummingbird	Colibrí Garganta de Rubí	M			
361	*Selasphorus flammula*	Volcano Hummingbird	Colibrí Chispita Volcanera (Chispita, Colibrí Mosca)	R-END			
362	*Selasphorus scintilla*	Scintillant Hummingbird	Colibrí Chispita Gorginaranja (Chispita, Colibrí Mosca)	R-END			
363	*Chlorostilbon canivetii*	Canivet's Emerald	Esmeralda Rabihorcada	R			
364	*Chlorostilbon assimilis*	Garden Emerald	Colibrí Esmeralda Jardinero	R-END			
365	*Klais guimeti*	Violet-headed Hummingbird	Colibrí Cabeciazul	R			

366	*Phaeochroa cuvierii*	Scaly-breasted Hummingbird	Colibrí Pechiescamado	R				
367	*Campylopterus hemileucurus*	Violet Sabrewing	Ala de Sable Violáceo	R				
368	*Eupherusa eximia*	Stripe-tailed Hummingbird	Colibrí Colirrayado	R				
369	*Eupherusa nigriventris*	Black-bellied Hummingbird	Colibrí Pechinegro	R-END				
370	*Elvira chionura*	White-tailed Emerald	Esmeralda Coliblanca	R-END				
371	*Elvira cupreiceps*	Coppery-headed Emerald	Esmeralda de Coronilla Cobriza	R-END				
372	*Microchera albocoronata*	Snowcap	Colibrí Copete de Nieve	R-END				
373	*Chalybura urochrysia*	Bronze-tailed Plumeleteer	Colibrí Patirrojo	R				
374	*Thalurania colombica*	Crowned Woodnymph	Colibrí Ninfa Verde-Violeta	R				
375	*Amazilia candida*	White-bellied Emerald	Amazilia Pechiblanca (Gorrión)	R?				
376	*Amazilia amabilis*	Blue-chested Hummingbird	Amazilia Pechiazul (Gorrión)	R				
377	*Amazilia decora*	Charming Hummingbird	Amazilia Corona de Berilo (Gorrión)	R-END				
378	*Amazilia boucardi*	Mangrove Hummingbird	Amazilia Manglera (Gorrión)	R-END				
379	*Amazilia cyanura*	Blue-tailed Hummingbird	Amazilia Coliazul (Gorrión)	R				
380	*Amazilia saucerottei*	Steely-vented Hummingbird	Amazilia Culiazul (Gorrión)	R				
381	*Amazilia edward*	Snowy-bellied Hummingbird	Amazilia Vientriblanca (Gorrión)	R-END				
382	*Amazilia tzacatl*	Rufous-tailed Hummingbird	Amazilia Rabirrufa (Gorrión)	R				
383	*Amazilia rutila*	Cinnamon Hummingbird	Amazilia Canela (Gorrión)	R				
384	*Lepidopyga coeruleogularis*	Sapphire-throated Hummingbird	Colibrí Garganta de Zafiro	R?				
385	*Hylocharis eliciae*	Blue-throated Goldentail	Colibrí Colidorado	R				

	Trogoniformes							
	Trogonidae (10)							
386	*Trogon clathratus*	Lattice-tailed Trogon	Trogón Ojiblanco	R-END				
387	*Trogon massena*	Slaty-tailed Trogon	Trogón Coliplomizo (Caicota)	R				
388	*Trogon melanocephalus*	Black-headed Trogon	Trogón Cabecinegro (Viuda Amarilla)	R				
389	*Trogon bairdii*	Baird's Trogon	Trogón Vientribermejo	R-END				
390	*Trogon caligatus*	Gartered Trogon	Trogón Violáceo AOCR	R				
391	*Trogon rufus*	Black-throated Trogon	Trogón Cabeciverde	R				
392	*Trogon elegans*	Elegant Trogon	Trogón Elegante (Viuda Roja)	R				
393	*Trogon collaris*	Collared Trogon	Trogón Collarejo (Viuda Roja, Quetzal Macho)	R				
394	*Trogon aurantiiventris*	Orange-bellied Trogon	Trogón Vientrianaranjado	R-END				
395	*Pharomachrus mocinno*	Resplendent Quetzal	Quetzal (Coludo)	R				
	Coraciiformes							
	Momotidae (6)							
396	*Hylomanes momotula*	Tody Motmot	Momoto Enano (Pájaro Bobo)	R				
397	*Momotus momota*	Blue-crowned Motmot	Momoto Común (Pájaro Bobo, Bobo Azul)	R				
398	*Baryphthengus martii*	Rufous Motmot	Momoto Canelo Mayor (Pájaro Bobo)	R				
399	*Electron carinatum*	Keel-billed Motmot	Momoto Pico Quilla (Pájaro Bobo)	R				
400	*Electron platyrhynchum*	Broad-billed Motmot	Momoto Piquiancho (Pájaro Bobo)	R				
401	*Eumomota superciliosa*	Turquoise-browed Motmot	Momoto Cejiceleste (Pájaro Bobo)	R				
	Alcedinidae (6)							
402	*Megaceryle torquatus*	Ringed Kingfisher	Martín Pescador Collarejo	R				
403	*Megaceryle alcyon*	Belted Kingfisher	Martín Pescador Norteño	M				
404	*Chloroceryle amazona*	Amazon Kingfisher	Martín Pescador Amazónico	R				
405	*Chloroceryle americana*	Green Kingfisher	Martín Pescador Verde	R				
406	*Chloroceryle inda*	Green-and-rufous Kingfisher	Martín Pescador Vientrirrufo	R				

407	*Chloroceryle aenea*	American Pygmy Kingfisher	Martín Pescador Enano	R				
	Piciformes							
	Bucconidae (5)							
408	*Notharchus hyperrhynchus*	White-necked Puffbird	Buco Collarejo	R				
409	*Notharchus tectus*	Pied Puffbird	Buco Pinto	R				
410	*Malacoptila panamensis*	White-whiskered Puffbird	Buco Barbón	R				
411	*Micromonacha lanceolata*	Lanceolated Monklet	Monjito Rayado	R				
412	*Monasa morphoeus*	White-fronted Nunbird	Monja Frentiblanca (Julío)	R				
	Galbulidae (2)							
413	*Galbula ruficauda*	Rufous-tailed Jacamar	Jacamar Rabirrufo (Gorrión de Montaña)	R				
414	*Jacamerops aureus*	Great Jacamar	Jacamar Grande	R				
	Capitonidae (1)							
415	*Eubucco bourcierii*	Red-headed Barbet	Barbudo Cabecirrojo (Ruano)	R				
	Semnornithidae (1)							
416	*Semnornis frantzii*	Prong-billed Barbet	Barbudo Cocora (Cocora, Carcareón)	R-END				
	Ramphastidae (6)							
417	*Aulacorhynchus prasinus*	Emerald Toucanet	Tucancillo Verde (Curré, Curré Verde)	R				
418	*Pteroglossus torquatus*	Collared Aracari	Tucancillo Collarejo (Cusingo, Tití, Félix)	R				
419	*Pteroglossus frantzii*	Fiery-billed Aracari	Tucancillo Piquianaranjado (Cusingo, Cachis, Filí)	R-END				
420	*Selenidera spectabilis*	Yellow-eared Toucanet	Tucancillo Orejiamarillo	R-END				
421	*Ramphastos sulfuratus*	Keel-billed Toucan	Tucán Pico Iris (Tucán Pico Arcoiris, Curré Negro)	R				
422	*Ramphastos ambiguus*	Black-mandibled Toucan	Tucán Pico Negro (Quioro, Dios te dé, Gran Curré Negro)	R				
	Picidae (16)							
423	*Picumnus olivaceus*	Olivaceous Piculet	Carpinterito Oliváceo (Telegrafista)	R				

424	*Melanerpes formicivorus*	Acorn Woodpecker	Carpintero Careto (Payasito)	R			
425	*Melanerpes chrysauchen*	Golden-naped Woodpecker	Capintero Nuquidorado	R-END			
426	*Melanerpes pucherani*	Black-cheeked Woodpecker	Carpintero Carinegro	R			
427	*Melanerpes rubricapillus*	Red-crowned Woodpecker	Carpintero Nuquirrojo	R			
428	*Melanerpes hoffmannii*	Hoffmann's Woodpecker	Carpintero de Hoffmann	R-END			
429	*Sphyrapicus varius*	Yellow-bellied Sapsucker	Carpintero Bebedor	M			
430	*Picoides fumigatus*	Smoky-brown Woodpecker	Carpintero Pardo	R			
431	*Picoides villosus*	Hairy Woodpecker	Carpintero Serranero o Velloso	R			
432	*Veniliornis kirkii*	Red-rumped Woodpecker	Carpintero Lomirrojo	R			
433	*Piculus simplex*	Rufous-winged Woodpecker	Carpintero Alirrufo	R-END			
434	*Colaptes rubiginosus*	Golden-olive Woodpecker	Carpintero Verde Dorado	R			
435	*Celeus loricatus*	Cinnamon Woodpecker	Carpintero Canelo	R			
436	*Celeus castaneus*	Chestnut-colored Woodpecker	Carpintero Castaño	R			
437	*Dryocopus lineatus*	Lineated Woodpecker	Carpintero Lineado	R			
438	*Campephilus guatemalensis*	Pale-billed Woodpecker	Carpintero Picoplata (Dos Golpes, Carpintero Chiricano)	R			
	Falconiformes						
	Falconidae (13)						
439	*Micrastur ruficollis*	Barred Forest-Falcon	Halcón de Monte Barreteado	R			
440	*Micrastur mirandollei*	Slaty-backed Forest-Falcon	Halcón de Monte Dorsigrís	R			
441	*Micrastur semitorquatus*	Collared Forest-Falcon	Halcón de Monte Collarejo	R			
442	*Ibycter americanus*	Red-throated Caracara	Caracara Avispera (Cacao, Come Cacao, Deslenguado)	R			

443	*Caracara cheriway*	Crested Caracara	Caracara Cargahuesos (Cargahuesos, Querque, Quebrantahuesos)	R			
444	*Milvago chimachima*	Yellow-headed Caracara	Caracara Cabecigualdo (Gavilán Blanco)	R			
445	*Herpetotheres cachinnans*	Laughing Falcon	Guaco	R			
446	*Falco sparverius*	American Kestrel	Cernícalo Americano (Klis-Klis, Camaleón)	M			
447	*Falco columbarius*	Merlin	Esmerejón	M			
448	*Falco femoralis*	Aplomado Falcon	Halcón Aplomado	M?			
449	*Falco rufigularis*	Bat Falcon	Halcón Cuelliblanco	R			
450	*Falco deiroleucus*	Orange-breasted Falcon	Halcón Pechirrufo	R?			
451	*Falco peregrinus*	Peregrine Falcon	Halcón Peregrino	M			
	Psittaciformes						
	Psittacidae (17)						
452	*Pyrrhura hoffmanni*	Sulphur-winged Parakeet	Perico Aliazufrado	R-END			
453	*Eupsittula nana*	Olive-throated Parakeet	Perico Azteco	R			
454	*Eupsittula canicularis*	Orange-fronted Parakeet	Perico Frentinaranja (Catano, Periquito, Zapoyol)	R			
455	*Eupsittula pertinax*	Brown-throated Parakeet	Perico Gorgicafé	R			
456	*Ara ambiguus*	Great Green Macaw	Guacamayo Verde Mayor (Lapa Verde)	R			
457	*Ara macao*	Scarlet Macaw	Guacamayo Rojo (Lapa Roja, Lapa Colorada)	R			
458	*Psittacara finschi*	Crimson-fronted Parakeet	Perico Frentirrojo (Cotorra, Chucuyo, Perico Colilarga o de Palmera)	R-END			
459	*Bolborhynchus lineola*	Barred Parakeet	Perico Listado	R			
460	*Brotogeris jugularis*	Orange-chinned Parakeet	Periquito Barbinaranja (Perico, Zapoyolito, Chimbolito, Catano)	R			
461	*Touit costaricensis*	Red-fronted Parrotlet	Periquito Alirrojo	R-END			
462	*Pyrilia haematotis*	Brown-hooded Parrot	Loro Cabecipardo (Lora)	R			
463	*Pionus menstruus*	Blue-headed Parrot	Loro Cabeciazul (Chucuyo)	R			

464	*Pionus senilis*	White-crowned Parrot	Loro Coroniblanco (Cotorra, Chucuyo)	R				
465	*Amazona albifrons*	White-fronted Parrot	Loro Frentiblanco (Cancan, Lora)	R				
466	*Amazona autumnalis*	Red-lored Parrot	Loro Frentirrojo (Lora Jupa Roja)	R				
467	*Amazona farinosa*	Mealy Parrot	Loro Verde (Lora Cabeza Negra, Lora Jupa Gris)	R				
468	*Amazona auropalliata*	Yellow-naped Parrot	Lora de Nuca Amarilla (Lora Jupa Amarilla)	R				
	Passeriformes							
	Thamnophilidae (22)							
469	*Cymbilaimus lineatus*	Fasciated Antshrike	Batará Lineado	R				
470	*Taraba major*	Great Antshrike	Batará Grande	R				
471	*Thamnophilus doliatus*	Barred Antshrike	Batará Barreteado	R				
472	*Thamnophilus bridgesi*	Black-hooded Antshrike	Batará Negruzco	R-END				
473	*Thamnophilus atrinucha*	Black-crowned Antshrike	Batará Plomizo	R				
474	*Thamnistes anabatinus*	Russet Antshrike	Batará Café	R				
475	*Dysithamnus mentalis*	Plain Antvireo	Batarito Cabecigrís	R				
476	*Dysithamnus striaticeps*	Streak-crowned Antvireo	Batarito Pechirrayado	R-END				
477	*Dysithamnus puncticeps*	Spot-crowned Antvireo	Batarito Cabecipunteado	R				
478	*Myrmotherula axillaris*	White-flanked Antwren	Hormiguerito Flanquiblanco	R				
479	*Myrmotherula schisticolor*	Slaty Antwren	Hormiguerito Pizarroso	R				
480	*Epinecrophylla fulviventris*	Checker-throated Antwren	Hormiguerito Café	R				
481	*Microrhopias quixensis*	Dot-winged Antwren	Hormiguerito Alipunteado	R				
482	*Euchrepomis callinota*	Rufous-rumped Antwren	Hormiguerito Lomirrufo	R				
483	*Cercomacra tyrannina*	Dusky Antbird	Hormiguero Negruzco	R				
484	*Gymnocichla nudiceps*	Bare-crowned Antbird	Hormiguero Calvo	R				

485	*Myrmeciza exsul*	Chestnut-backed Antbird	Hormiguero Dorsicastaño	R			
486	*Myrmeciza laemosticta*	Dull-mantled Antbird	Hormiguero Alimaculado	R			
487	*Myrmeciza zeledoni*	Zeledon's Antbird	Hormiguero de Zeledón	R			
488	*Hylophylax naevioides*	Spotted Antbird	Hormiguero Moteado	R			
489	*Gymnopithys bicolor*	Bicolored Antbird	Hormiguero Bicolor	R			
490	*Phaenostictus mcleannani*	Ocellated Antbird	Hormiguero Ocelado	R			
	Conopophagidae (1)						
491	*Pittasoma michleri*	Black-crowned Antpitta	Tororoi Pechiescamoso (Hormiguero)	R-END			
	Grallariidae (4)						
492	*Grallaria guatimalensis*	Scaled Antpitta	Tororoi Dorsiescamado (Hormiguero)	R			
493	*Hylopezus perspicillatus*	Streak-chested Antpitta	Tororoi Pechilistado (Hormiguero)	R			
494	*Hylopezus dives*	Thicket Antpitta	Tororoi Pechicanelo (Hormiguero)	R-END			
495	*Grallaricula flavirostris*	Ochre-breasted Antpitta	Tororoi Piquigualdo (Hormiguero)	R			
	Rhinocryptidae (1)						
496	*Scytalopus argentifrons*	Silvery-fronted Tapaculo	Tapaculo Frentiplateado	R-END			
	Formicariidae (3)						
497	*Formicarius analis*	Black-faced Antthrush	Gallito Hormiguero Carinegro	R			
498	*Formicarius nigricapillus*	Black-headed Antthrush	Gallito Hormiguero Cabecinegro	R			
499	*Formicarius rufipectus*	Rufous-breasted Antthrush	Gallito Hormiguero Pechicastaño	R			
	Furnariidae (34)						
500	*Sclerurus mexicanus*	Tawny-throated Leaftosser	Tirahojas Pechirrufo	R			
501	*Sclerurus albigularis*	Gray-throated Leaftosser	Tirahojas Gargantigrís	R			
502	*Sclerurus guatemalensis*	Scaly-throated Leaftosser	Tirahojas Barbiescamado	R			

503	*Sittasomus griseicapillus*	Olivaceous Woodcreeper	Trepadorcito Aceitunado	R				
504	*Deconychura longicauda*	Long-tailed Woodcreeper	Trepador Delgado	R				
505	*Dendrocincla homochroa*	Ruddy Woodcreeper	Trepador Rojizo	R				
506	*Dendrocincla anabatina*	Tawny-winged Woodcreeper	Trepador Alirrubio	R				
507	*Dendrocincla fuliginosa*	Plain-brown Woodcreeper	Trepador Pardo	R				
508	*Glyphorhynchus spirurus*	Wedge-billed Woodcreeper	Trepadorcito Pico de Cuña	R				
509	*Dendrocolaptes sanctithomae*	Northern-barred Woodcreeper	Trepador Barreteado	R				
510	*Dendrocolaptes picumnus*	Black-banded Woodcreeper	Trepador Vientribarreteado	R				
511	*Xiphocolaptes promeropirhynchus*	Strong-billed Woodcreeper	Trepador Gigante	R				
512	*Xiphorhynchus susurrans*	Cocoa Woodcreeper	Trepador Gorgianteado	R				
513	*Xiphorhynchus flavigaster*	Ivory-billed Woodcreeper	Trepador Piquiclaro	R				
514	*Xiphorhynchus lachrymosus*	Black-striped Woodcreeper	Trepador Pinto (Relinchero)	R				
515	*Xiphorhynchus erythropygius*	Spotted Woodcreeper	Trepador Manchado	R				
516	*Campylorhamphus pusillus*	Brown-billed Scythebill	Trepador Pico de Hoz	R				
517	*Lepidocolaptes souleyetii*	Streak-headed Woodcreeper	Trepador Cabecirrayado	R				
518	*Lepidocolaptes affinis*	Spot-crowned Woodcreeper	Trepador Cabecipunteado	R				
519	*Xenops minutus*	Plain Xenops	Xenops Común	R				
520	*Xenops rutilans*	Streaked Xenops	Xenops Rayado	R				
521	*Pseudocolaptes lawrencii*	Buffy Tuftedcheek	Trepamusgo Cachetón	R				
522	*Philydor rufum*	Buff-fronted Foliage-gleaner	Trepamusgo Rojizo	R				
523	*Anabacerthia variegaticeps*	Scaly-throated Foliage-gleaner	Trepamusgo de Anteojos	R				

524	*Syndactyla subalaris*	Lineated Foliage-gleaner	Trepamusgo Lineado	R			
525	*Clibanornis rubiginosus*	Ruddy Foliage-gleaner	Hojarrasquero Rojizo	R			
526	*Thripadectes rufobrunneus*	Streak-breasted Treehunter	Trepamusgo Cuellirojizo	R-END			
527	*Automolus ochrolaemus*	Buff-throated Foliage-gleaner	Hojarrasquero Gorgianteado	R			
528	*Automolus subulatus*	Striped Woodhunter	Trepamusgo Rayado	R			
529	*Premnoplex brunnescens*	Spotted Barbtail	Subepalo Moteado	R			
530	*Margarornis rubiginosus*	Ruddy Treerunner	Subepalo Rojizo (Chupamusgo)	R-END			
531	*Cranioleuca erythrops*	Red-faced Spinetail	Colaespina Carirroja	R			
532	*Synallaxis albescens*	Pale-breasted Spinetail	Arquitecto Güitío	R			
533	*Synallaxis brachyura*	Slaty Spinetail	Arquitecto Plomizo	R			
	Tyrannidae (83)						
534	*Ornithion semiflavum*	Yellow-bellied Tyrannulet	Mosquerito Cejiblanco	R			
535	*Ornithion brunneicapillus*	Brown-capped Tyrannulet	Mosquerito Gorricafé	R			
536	*Camptostoma imberbe*	Northern Beardless-Tyrannulet	Mosquerito Chillón	R, M?			
537	*Camptostoma obsoletum*	Southern Beardless-Tyrannulet	Mosquerito Silbador	R			
538	*Phaeomyias murina*	Mouse-colored Tyrannulet	Mosquerito Cafecito	R			
539	*Nesotriccus ridgwayi*	Cocos Flycatcher	Mosquerito de la Isla del Coco	R-END			
540	*Capsiempis flaveola*	Yellow Tyrannulet	Mosquerito Amarillo	R			
541	*Tyrannulus elatus*	Yellow-crowned Tyrannulet	Mosquerito Coroniamarillo	R			
542	*Myiopagis viridicata*	Greenish Elaenia	Elainia Verdosa (Tontillo)	R			
543	*Elaenia flavogaster*	Yellow-bellied Elaenia	Elainia Copetona (Tontillo, Bobillo, Copetoncillo)	R			
544	*Elaenia chiriquensis*	Lesser Elaenia	Elainia Sabanera (Tontillo)	R			

545	*Elaenia frantzii*	Mountain Elaenia	Elainia Montañera (Tontillo, Bobillo)	R			
546	*Serpophaga cinerea*	Torrent Tyrannulet	Mosquerito Guardarrios	R			
547	*Mionectes olivaceus*	Olive-striped Flycatcher	Mosquerito Ojimanchado (Tontillo)	R			
548	*Mionectes oleagineus*	Ochre-bellied Flycatcher	Mosquerito Aceitunado (Tontillo)	R			
549	*Leptopogon amaurocephalus*	Sepia-capped Flycatcher	Mosquerito Cabecipardo	R			
550	*Leptopogon superciliaris*	Slaty-capped Flycatcher	Mosquerito Orejinegro	R			
551	*Phylloscartes superciliaris*	Rufous-browed Tyrannulet	Mosquerito Cejirrufo	R			
552	*Phyllomyias burmeisteri*	Rough-legged Tyrannulet	Mosquerito Frentiblanco	R			
553	*Zimmerius vilissimus*	Paltry Tyrannulet	Mosquerito Cejigrís	R			
554	*Sublegatus arenarum*	Northern Scrub-Flycatcher	Mosquero Gorgigrís	R			
555	*Myiornis atricapillus*	Black-capped Pygmy-Tyrant	Mosquerito Colicorto	R			
556	*Lophotriccus pileatus*	Scale-crested Pygmy-Tyrant	Mosquerito de Yelmo	R			
557	*Oncostoma cinereigulare*	Northern Bentbill	Piquitorcido Norteño (Brujita)	R			
558	*Poecilotriccus sylvia*	Slate-headed Tody-Flycatcher	Espatulilla Cabecigrís	R			
559	*Todirostrum cinereum*	Common Tody-Flycatcher	Espatulilla Común (Espatulilla, Mantequillilla)	R			
560	*Todirostrum nigriceps*	Black-headed Tody-Flycatcher	Espatulilla Cabecinegra	R			
561	*Rhynchocyclus brevirostris*	Eye-ringed Flatbill	Piquiplano de Anteojos	R			
562	*Tolmomyias sulphurescens*	Yellow-olive Flycatcher	Piquiplano Azufrado	R			
563	*Tolmomyias assimilis*	Yellow-margined Flycatcher	Piquiplano Aliamarillo	R			
564	*Platyrinchus cancrominus*	Stub-tailed Spadebill	Piquichato Norteño	R			
565	*Platyrinchus mystaceus*	White-throated Spadebill	Piquichato Gargantiblanco	R			

566	*Platyrinchus coronatus*	Golden-crowned Spadebill	Piquichato Coronirrufo	R			
567	*Onychorhynchus coronatus*	Royal Flycatcher	Mosquero Real	R			
568	*Terenotriccus erythrurus*	Ruddy-tailed Flycatcher	Mosquerito Colirrufo	R			
569	*Myiobius sulphureipygius*	Sulphur-rumped Flycatcher	Mosquerito Lomiamarillo	R			
570	*Myiobius atricaudus*	Black-tailed Flycatcher	Mosquerito Colinegro	R			
571	*Myiophobus fasciatus*	Bran-colored Flycatcher	Mosquerito Pechirrayado	R			
572	*Aphanotriccus capitalis*	Tawny-chested Flycatcher	Mosquerito Pechileonado	R-END			
573	*Mitrephanes phaeocercus*	Tufted Flycatcher	Mosquerito Moñudo	R			
574	*Contopus cooperi*	Olive-sided Flycatcher	Pibí Boreal (Tontillo)	M			
575	*Contopus lugubris*	Dark Pewee	Pibí Sombrío (Tontillo)	R-END			
576	*Contopus ochraceus*	Ochraceous Pewee	Pibí Ocráceo (Tontillo)	R-END			
577	*Contopus sordidulus*	Western Wood-Pewee	Pibí Occidental (Tontillo, Piguí)	M, R?			
578	*Contopus virens*	Eastern Wood-Pewee	Pibí Oriental (Tontillo, Piguí)	M			
579	*Contopus cinereus*	Tropical Pewee	Pibí Tropical (Tontillo, Piguí)	R			
580	*Empidonax flaviventris*	Yellow-bellied Flycatcher	Mosquerito Vientriamarillo	M			
581	*Empidonax virescens*	Acadian Flycatcher	Mosquerito Verdoso	M			
582	*Empidonax alnorum*	Alder Flycatcher	Mosquerito de Charral	M			
583	*Empidonax traillii*	Willow Flycatcher	Mosquerito de Traill	M			
584	*Empidonax albigularis*	White-throated Flycatcher	Mosquerito Gargantiblanco	R, M			
585	*Empidonax minimus*	Least Flycatcher	Mosquerito Chebec	M			
586	*Empidonax flavescens*	Yellowish Flycatcher	Mosquerito Amarillento	R			
587	*Empidonax atriceps*	Black-capped Flycatcher	Mosquerito Cabecinegro	R-END			
588	*Sayornis nigricans*	Black Phoebe	Mosquero de Agua	R			
589	*Sayornis phoebe*	Eastern Phoebe	Mosquero Fibí	A			

590	*Pyrocephalus rubinus*	Vermilion Flycatcher	Mosquerito Rojo	A				
591	*Colonia colonus*	Long-tailed Tyrant	Mosquero Coludo	R				
592	*Attila spadiceus*	Bright-rumped Attila	Atila Lomiamarilla	R				
593	*Rhytipterna holerythra*	Rufous Mourner	Plañidera Rojiza	R				
594	*Myiarchus tuberculifer*	Dusky-capped Flycatcher	Copetón Crestioscuro (Tontillo)	R				
595	*Myiarchus panamensis*	Panama Flycatcher	Copetón Colipardo (Tontillo)	R				
596	*Myiarchus cinerascens*	Ash-throated Flycatcher	Copetón Garganticeniza (Tontillo)	A				
597	*Myiarchus nuttingi*	Nutting's Flycatcher	Copetón de Nutting (Tontillo)	R				
598	*Myiarchus crinitus*	Great Crested Flycatcher	Copetón Viajero (Tontillo)	M				
599	*Myiarchus tyrannulus*	Brown-crested Flycatcher	Copetón Crestipardo (Tontillo)	R				
600	*Pitangus sulphuratus*	Great Kiskadee	Bienteveo Grande (Cristo Fue, Pecho Amarillo)	R				
601	*Megarhynchus pitangua*	Boat-billed Flycatcher	Mosquerón Picudo (Pecho Amarillo)	R				
602	*Myiozetetes cayanensis*	Rusty-margined Flycatcher	Mosquero Alicastaño (Pecho Amarillo)	R				
603	*Myiozetetes similis*	Social Flycatcher	Mosquero Cejiblanco (Pecho Amarillo)	R				
604	*Myiozetetes granadensis*	Gray-capped Flycatcher	Mosquero Cabecigrís (Pecho Amarillo)	R				
605	*Conopias albovittatus*	White-ringed Flycatcher	Mosquero Cabecianillado (Pecho Amarillo)	R				
606	*Myiodynastes hemichrysus*	Golden-bellied Flycatcher	Mosquero Vientridorado (Pecho Amarillo)	R-END				
607	*Myiodynastes maculatus*	Streaked Flycatcher	Mosquero Listado (Pecho Amarillo)	R, RR, M				
608	*Myiodynastes luteiventris*	Sulphur-bellied Flycatcher	Mosquero Vientriazufrado (Pecho Amarillo)	RR, M				
609	*Legatus leucophaius*	Piratic Flycatcher	Mosquero Pirata (Pecho Amarillo)	RR, M				
610	*Tyrannus melancholicus*	Tropical Kingbird	Tirano Tropical (Pecho Amarillo)	R				

611	*Tyrannus verticalis*	Western Kingbird	Tirano Occidental (Pecho Amarillo)	M			
612	*Tyrannus tyrannus*	Eastern Kingbird	Tirano Norteño (Viuda Negra)	M			
613	*Tyrannus dominicensis*	Gray Kingbird	Tirano Gris	M			
614	*Tyrannus forficatus*	Scissor-tailed Flycatcher	Tijereta Rosada (Tijerilla)	M			
615	*Tyrannus savana*	Fork-tailed Flycatcher	Tijereta Sabanera (Tijerilla)	R, M?			
	Genus Incertae Sedis						
616	*Piprites griseiceps*	Gray-headed Piprites	Saltarín Cabecigrís	R			
	Tytiridae (9)						
617	*Schiffornis veraepacis*	Northern Schiffornis	Tordo-saltarín	R			
618	*Laniocera rufescens*	Speckled Mourner	Plañidera Moteada	R			
619	*Tityra semifasciata*	Masked Tityra	Tityra Carirroja (Pájaro Chancho, Calandria)	R			
620	*Tityra inquisitor*	Black-crowned Tityra	Tityra Coroninegra (Pájaro Chancho)	R			
621	*Pachyramphus versicolor*	Barred Becard	Cabezón Ondeado	R			
622	*Pachyramphus cinnamomeus*	Cinnamon Becard	Cabezón Canelo	R			
623	*Pachyramphus polychopterus*	White-winged Becard	Cabezón Aliblanco	R			
624	*Pachyramphus albogriseus*	Black-and-white Becard	Cabezón Cejiblanco	R			
625	*Pachyramphus aglaiae*	Rose-throated Becard	Cabezón Plomizo	R			
	Cotingidae (8)						
626	*Querula purpurata*	Purple-throated Fruitcrow	Querula Gorgimorada	R			
627	*Cephalopterus glabricollis*	Bare-necked Umbrellabird	Pájaro-sombrilla Cuellinudo (Pájaro Danta)	R-END			
628	*Cotinga amabilis*	Lovely Cotinga	Cotinga Linda	R			
629	*Cotinga ridgwayi*	Turquoise Cotinga	Cotinga Turquesa	R-END			
630	*Lipaugus unirufus*	Rufous Piha	Piha Rojiza	R			
631	*Procnias tricarunculatus*	Three-wattled Bellbird	Campanero Tricarunculado (Pájaro Campana, Rin-Ran, Calandria)	R-END			

632	*Carpodectes antoniae*	Yellow-billed Cotinga	Cotinga Piquiamarillo	R-END				
633	*Carpodectes nitidus*	Snowy Cotinga	Cotinga Blanca	R-END				
	Pipridae (8)							
634	*Chiroxiphia lanceolata*	Lance-tailed Manakin	Saltarín Coludo (Toledo)	R				
635	*Chiroxiphia linearis*	Long-tailed Manakin	Saltarín Toledo (Toledo)	R				
636	*Corapipo altera*	White-ruffed Manakin	Saltarín Gorgiblanco	R				
637	*Lepidothrix coronata*	Blue-crowned Manakin	Saltarín Coroniceleste	R				
638	*Manacus candei*	White-collared Manakin	Saltarín Cuelliblanco (Quiebrapalos, Quiebraramas, Bailarín)	R				
639	*Manacus aurantiacus*	Orange-collared Manakin	Saltarín Cuellinaranja (Quiebrapalos, Hombrecillo)	R-END				
640	*Dixiphia pipra*	White-crowned Manakin	Saltarín Coroniblanco	R				
641	*Ceratopipra mentalis*	Red-capped Manakin	Saltarín Cabecirrojo	R				
	Oxyruncidae (1)							
642	*Oxyruncus cristatus*	Sharpbill	Picoagudo	R				
	Vireonidae (16)							
643	*Vireo griseusA*	White-eyed Vireo	Vireo Ojiblanco	M				
644	*Vireo pallensO*	Mangrove Vireo	Vireo de Manglar	R				
645	*Vireo flavifronsC*	Yellow-throated Vireo	Vireo Pechiamarillo	M				
646	*Vireo solitariusR*	Blue-headed Vireo	Vireo Solitario	M				
647	*Vireo carmioli*	Yellow-winged Vireo	Vireo Aliamarillo	R-END				
648	*Vireo gilvus*	Warbling Vireo	Vireo Canoro	M				
649	*Vireo leucophrys*	Brown-capped Vireo	Vireo Montañero	R				
650	*Vireo philadelphicus*	Philadelphia Vireo	Vireo Amarillento	M				
651	*Vireo olivaceus*	Red-eyed Vireo	Vireo Ojirrojo (Chiguisa)	M				
652	*Vireo flavoviridis*	Yellow-green Vireo	Vireo Cabecigrís (Chiguisa, Chuesa, Cazadora, Fraile)	RR, M				

653	*Vireo altiloquus*	Black-whiskered Vireo	Vireo Bigotudo	M			
654	*Hylophilus flavipes*	Scrub Greenlet	Verdillo Matorralero	R			
655	*Hylophilus ochraceiceps*	Tawny-crowned Greenlet	Verdillo Leonado	R			
656	*Hylophilus decurtatus*	Lesser Greenlet	Verdillo Menudo	R			
657	*Vireolanius pulchellus*	Green Shrike-Vireo	Vireón Esmeraldino	R			
658	*Cyclarhis gujanensis*	Rufous-browed Peppershrike	Vireón Cejirrufo	R			
	Corvidae (5)						
659	*Cyanolyca argentigula*	Silvery-throated Jay	Urraca Gorgiplateada	R-END			
660	*Cyanolyca cucullata*	Azure-hooded Jay	Urraca de Toca Celeste (Piapia de Montaña)	R			
661	*Calocitta formosa*	White-throated Magpie-Jay	Urraca Copetona (Urraca, Piapia Azul)	R			
662	*Psilorhinus morio*	Brown Jay	Urraca Parda (Piapia)	R			
663	*Cyanocorax affinis*	Black-chested Jay	Urraca Pechinegra	R			
	Hirundinidae (13)						
664	*Progne subis*	Purple Martin	Martín Purpúrea (Golondrón)	M			
665	*Progne chalybea*	Gray-breasted Martin	Martín Pechigrís	R			
666	*Progne tapera*	Brown-chested Martin	Martín de Ríos (Golondrina)	M			
667	*Tachycineta bicolor*	Tree Swallow	Golondrina Bicolor	M			
668	*Tachycineta albilinea*	Mangrove Swallow	Golondrina Lomiblanca	R			
669	*Tachycineta thalassina*	Violet-green Swallow	Golondrina Verdiviolácea	M			
670	*Pygochelidon cyanoleuca*	Blue-and-white Swallow	Golondrina Azul y Blanco	R, M			
671	*Stelgidopteryx serripennis*	Northern Rough-winged Swallow	Golondrina Alirrasposa Norteña	R, M			
672	*Stelgidopteryx ruficollis*	Southern Rough-winged Swallow	Golondrina Alirrasposa Sureña	R			
673	*Riparia riparia*	Bank Swallow	Golondrina Ribereña	M			
674	*Petrochelidon pyrrhonota*	Cliff Swallow	Golondrina Risquera	M			
675	*Petrochelidon fulva*	Cave Swallow	Golondrina Cavernícola	A			
676	*Hirundo rustica*	Barn Swallow	Golondrina Tijereta	M			

	Troglodytidae (22)							
677	*Salpinctes obsoletus*	Rock Wren	Soterrey Roquero	R				
678	*Microcerculus philomela*	Nightingale Wren	Soterrey Ruiseñor	R				
679	*Microcerculus marginatus*	Scaly-breasted Wren	Soterrey Silbador	R				
680	*Troglodytes aedon*	House Wren	Soterrey Cucarachero (Soterrey, Soterré)	R				
681	*Troglodytes ochraceus*	Ochraceous Wren	Soterrey Ocroso	R-END				
682	*Thryorchilus browni*	Timberline Wren	Soterrey del Bambú	R-END				
683	*Cistothorus platensis*	Sedge Wren	Soterrey Sabanero (Guachipelín)	R				
684	*Campylorhynchus zonatus*	Band-backed Wren	Soterrey Matraquero	R				
685	*Campylorhynchus rufinucha*	Rufous-naped Wren	Soterrey Nuquirrufo (Chico Piojo, Botijón, Salta Piñuela)	R				
686	*Pheugopedius atrogularis*	Black-throated Wren	Soterrey Gorginegro	R-END				
687	*Pheugopedius rutilus*	Rufous-breasted Wren	Soterrey Carimoteado	R				
688	*Pheugopedius maculipectus*	Spot-breasted Wren	Soterrey Pechimoteado	R				
689	*Pheugopedius fasciatoventris*	Black-bellied Wren	Soterrey Vientrinegro	R-END				
690	*Thryophilus rufalbus*	Rufous-and-white Wren	Soterrey Rufo y Blanco	R				
691	*Thryophilus pleurostictus*	Banded Wren	Soterrey de Costillas Barreteadas	R				
692	*Cantorchilus thoracicus*	Stripe-breasted Wren	Soterrey Pechirrayado	R-END				
693	*Cantorchilus modestus*	Plain Wren	Soterrey Chinchirigüí (Huevos Blancos)	R				
694	*Cantorchilus nigricapillus*	Bay Wren	Soterrey Castaño	R				
695	*Cantorchilus semibadius*	Riverside Wren	Soterrey Pechibarreteado	R-END				
696	*Henicorhina leucosticta*	White-breasted Wood-Wren	Soterrey de Selva Pechiblanco	R				
697	*Henicorhina leucophrys*	Gray-breasted Wood-Wren	Soterrey de Selva Pechigrís	R				

698	*Cyphorhinus phaeocephalus*	Song Wren	Soterrey Canoro	R			
	Polioptilidae (4)						
699	*Microbates cinereiventris*	Tawny-faced Gnatwren	Soterillo Caricafé	R			
700	*Ramphocaenus melanurus*	Long-billed Gnatwren	Soterillo Picudo	R			
701	*Polioptila albiloris*	White-lored Gnatcatcher	Perlita Cabecinegra (Espatulilla, Cazadora)	R			
702	*Polioptila plumbea*	Tropical Gnatcather	Perlita Tropical (Espatulilla, Cazadora)	R			
	Cinclidae (1)						
703	*Cinclus mexicanus*	American Dipper	Mirlo Acuático Plomizo	R			
	Turdidae (15)						
704	*Myadestes melanops*	Black-faced Solitaire	Solitario Carinegro (Jilguero)	R-END			
705	*Catharus gracilirostris*	Black-billed Nightingale-Thrush	Zorzal Piquinegro (Cuitiento)	R-END			
706	*Catharus aurantiirostris*	Orange-billed Nightingale-Thrush	Zorzal Piquianaranjado (Jilguerillo de Charral, Inglesito)	R			
707	*Catharus fuscater*	Slaty-backed Nightingale-Thrush	Zorzal Sombrío (Arremedón, Arremendado, Jilguerillo)	R			
708	*Catharus frantzii*	Ruddy-capped Nightingale-Thrush	Zorzal Gorrirojizo (Jilguerillo de Montaña, Jilguerillo de Ronda)	R			
709	*Catharus mexicanus*	Black-headed Nightingale-Thrush	Zorzal Cabecinegro	R			
710	*Catharus fuscescens*	Veery	Zorzal Dorsirrojizo (Conchita)	M			
711	*Catharus minimus*	Gray-cheeked Thrush	Zorzal Carigrís (Conchita)	M			
712	*Catharus ustulatus*	Swainson's Thrush	Zorzal de Swainson (Conchita)	M			
713	*Hylocichla mustelina*	Wood Thrush	Zorzal del Bosque	M			
714	*Turdus nigrescens*	Sooty Thrush	Mirlo Negruzco (Yigüirro Escarchero, Escarchado)	R-END			
715	*Turdus plebejus*	Mountain Thrush	Mirlo Montañero (Yigüirro de Montaña)	R			
716	*Turdus obsoletus*	Pale-vented Thrush	Mirlo Vientriblanco (Yigüirro de Montaña)	R			
717	*Turdus grayi*	Clay-colored Thrush	Mirlo Pardo (Yigüirro)	R			

718	*Turdus assimilis*	White-throated Thrush	Mirlo Gorgiblanco (Yigüirro Collarejo, Yigüirro de Montaña)	R				
	Mimidae (2)							
719	*Dumetella carolinensis*	Gray Catbird	Pájaro-gato Gris	M				
720	*Mimus gilvus*	Tropical Mockingbird	Pájaro-imitador Tropical	R				
	Motacillidae (1)							
721	*Anthus rubescens*	American Pipit	Bisbita Americana	A				
	Bombycillidae (1)							
722	*Bombycilla cedrorum*	Cedar Waxwing	Ampelis Americano (Jilguero Chino)	M				
	Ptiliogonatidae (2)							
723	*Phainoptila melanoxantha*	Black-and-yellow Silky-Flycatcher	Capulinero Negro y Amarillo (Comemoras)	R-END				
724	*Ptiliogonys caudatus*	Long-tailed Silky-Flycatcher	Capulinero Colilargo (Pitorreal, Timbre, Coronel)	R-END				
	Parulidae (53)							
725	*Seiurus aurocapilla*	Ovenbird	Reinita Hornera	M				
726	*Helmitheros vermivorum*	Worm-eating Warbler	Reinita Gusanera	M				
727	*Parkesia motacilla*	Louisiana Waterthrush	Reinita Acuática Piquigrande (Menea Cola, Tordo de Agua)	M				
728	*Parkesia noveboracensis*	Northern Waterthrush	Reinita Acuática Norteña (Menea Cola, Tordo de Agua)	M				
729	*Vermivora chrysoptera*	Golden-winged Warbler	Reinita Alidorada	M				
730	*Vermivora cyanoptera*	Blue-winged Warbler	Reinita Aliazul	M				
731	*Mniotilta varia*	Black-and-white Warbler	Reinita Trepadora (Zebrita)	M				
732	*Protonotaria citrea*	Prothonotary Warbler	Reinita Cabecidorada	M				
733	*Oreothlypis gutturalis*	Flame-throated Warbler	Reinita Garganta de Fuego	R-END				
734	*Oreothlypis peregrina*	Tennessee Warbler	Reinita Verdilla (Cazadorcita)	M				
735	*Oreothlypis celata*	Orange-crowned Warbler	Reinita Olivácea	M- SC				
736	*Oreothlypis ruficapilla*	Nashville Warbler	Reinita Cachetigrís	M				

737	*Oporornis agilis*	Connecticut Warbler	Reinita Ojianillada	A- SC			
738	*Geothlypis poliocephala*	Gray-crowned Yellowthroat	Antifacito Coronigrís	R			
739	*Geothlypis aequinoctialis*	Masked Yellowthroat	Antifacito Sureño	R			
740	*Geothlypis tolmiei*	MacGillivray's Warbler	Reinita de Tupidero	M			
741	*Geothlypis philadelphia*	Mourning Warbler	Reinita Enlutada	M			
742	*Geothlypis formosa*	Kentucky Warbler	Reinita Cachetinegra	M			
743	*Geothlypis semiflava*	Olive-crowned Yellowthroat	Antifacito Coroniolivo	R			
744	*Geothlypis trichas*	Common Yellowthroat	Antifacito Norteño	M			
745	*Setophaga citrina*	Hooded Warbler	Reinita Encapuchada	M			
746	*Setophaga ruticilla*	American Redstart	Candelita Norteña (Raya Roja)	M			
747	*Setophaga tigrina*	Cape May Warbler	Reinita Tigrina	M			
748	*Setophaga cerulea*	Cerulean Warbler	Reinita Cerulea	M			
749	*Setophaga americana*	Northern Parula	Parula Norteña	M			
750	*Setophaga pitiayumi*	Tropical Parula	Parula Tropical	R			
751	*Setophaga magnolia*	Magnolia Warbler	Reinita Colifajeada	M			
752	*Setophaga castanea*	Bay-breasted Warbler	Reinita Castaña	M			
753	*Setophaga fusca*	Blackburnian Warbler	Reinita Gorginaranja	M			
754	*Setophaga petechia*	Yellow Warbler	Reinita Amarilla (Canarita)	R, M			
755	*Setophaga pensylvanica*	Chestnut-sided Warbler	Reinita de Costillas Castañas	M			
756	*Setophaga striata*	Blackpoll Warbler	Reinita Rayada	M			
757	*Setophaga caerulescens*	Black-throated Blue Warbler	Reinita Azul y Negro	M			
758	*Setophaga palmarum*	Palm Warbler	Reinita Coronicastaña	M			
759	*Setophaga pinus*	Pine Warbler	Reinita de Pinos	M- SC			
760	*Setophaga coronata*	Yellow-rumped Warbler	Reinita Lomiamarilla	M			
761	*Setophaga dominica*	Yellow-throated Warbler	Reinita Gorgiamarilla	M			
762	*Setophaga discolor*	Prairie Warbler	Reinita Galana	M			

763	*Setophaga townsendi*	Townsend's Warbler	Reinita de Townsend	M			
764	*Setophaga occidentalis*	Hermit Warbler	Reinita Cabecigualda	M			
765	*Setophaga chrysoparia*	Golden-cheeked Warbler	Reinita Caridorada	M- SC			
766	*Setophaga virens*	Black-throated Green Warbler	Reinita Cariamarilla	M			
767	*Myiothlypis fulvicauda*	Buff-rumped Warbler	Reinita Guardaribera (Cola Amarilla)	R			
768	*Basileuterus rufifrons*	Rufous-capped Warbler	Reinita Cabecicastaña	R			
769	*Basileuterus melanogenys*	Black-cheeked Warbler	Reinita Carinegra	R-END			
770	*Basileuterus culicivorus*	Golden-crowned Warbler	Reinita Coronidorada	R			
771	*Basileuterus tristriatus*	Three-striped Warbler	Reinita Cabecilistada	R			
772	*Cardellina canadensis*	Canada Warbler	Reinita Pechirrayada	M			
773	*Cardellina pusilla*	Wilson's Warbler	Reinita Gorrinegra (Curruquita)	M			
774	*Myioborus miniatus*	Slate-throated Redstart	Candelita Pechinegra (Candelita)	R			
775	*Myioborus torquatus*	Collared Redstart	Candelita Collareja (Amigo de Hombre)	R-END			
776	*Zeledonia coronata*	Wrenthrush	Zeledonia	R-END			
777	*Icteria virens*	Yellow-breasted Chat	Reinita Grande	M			
	Thraupidae (51)						
778	*Bangsia arcaei*	Blue-and-gold Tanager	Tangara de Costillas Negras (Agüión)	R-END			
779	*Thraupis episcopus*	Blue-gray Tanager	Tangara Azuleja (Viudita, Viuda)	R			
780	*Thraupis abbas*	Yellow-winged Tanager	Tangara Aliamarilla	R?			
781	*Thraupis palmarum*	Palm Tanager	Tangara Palmera (Viudita de la Costa)	R			
782	*Tangara larvata*	Golden-hooded Tanager	Tangara Capuchidorada (Juana, Mariposa, Siete Colores)	R			
783	*Tangara guttata*	Speckled Tanager	Tangara Moteada (Cebra)	R			
784	*Tangara dowii*	Spangle-cheeked Tanager	Tangara Vientricastaña (Mariposa de Clima Frío)	R-END			

785	*Tangara inornata*	Plain-colored Tanager	Tangara Cenicienta	R-END				
786	*Tangara lavinia*	Rufous-winged Tanager	Tangara Alirrufa	R				
787	*Tangara gyrola*	Bay-headed Tanager	Tangara Cabecicastaña (Pavito)	R				
788	*Tangara florida*	Emerald Tanager	Tangara Orejinegra	R				
789	*Tangara icterocephala*	Silver-throated Tanager	Tangara Dorada (Rayo de Sol, Chia, Juanita)	R				
790	*Sicalis luteola*	Grassland Yellow-Finch	Chirigue Sabanero	A				
791	*Haplospiza rustica*	Slaty Finch	Fringilo Plomizo (Semillero)	R				
792	*Acanthidops bairdi*	Peg-billed Finch	Fringilo Piquiagudo (Semillero)	R-END				
793	*Diglossa plumbea*	Slaty Flowerpiercer	Pinchaflor Plomizo	R-END				
794	*Chlorophanes spiza*	Green Honeycreeper	Mielero Verde (Rey de Mar, Verde Mar, Rey de Trepadores)	R				
795	*Chrysothlypis chrysomelas*	Black-and-yellow Tanager	Tangara Negro y Dorado	R-END				
796	*Heterospingus rubrifrons*	Sulphur-rumped Tanager	Tangara Lomiazufrada	R-END				
797	*Volatinia jacarinaA*	Blue-black Grassquit	Semillerito Negro Azulado (Brea, Pius, Piusillo Negro, Saltapalito)	R				
798	*Eucometis penicillata*	Gray-headed Tanager	Tangara Cabecigrís	R				
799	*Tachyphonus luctuosus*	White-shouldered Tanager	Tangara Caponiblanca	R				
800	*Tachyphonus delattrii*	Tawny-crested Tanager	Tangara Coronidorada	R				
801	*Tachyphonus rufus*	White-lined Tanager	Tangara Forriblanca (Fraile)	R				
802	*Lanio leucothorax*	White-throated Shrike-Tanager	Tangara Piquiganchuda	R-END				
803	*Ramphocelus sanguinolentus*	Crimson-collared Tanager	Tangara Capuchirroja (Rey de Sargento, Sangre de Toro)	R				
804	*Ramphocelus passerinii*	Passerini's Tanager	Tangara de Passerini (Sargento, Rabadilla Tinta, Terciopelo, Sangre de Toro)	R				
805	*Ramphocelus costaricensis*	Cherries's Tanager	Tangara de Cherrie, Tangara Costarricense (Sargento)	R-END				

806	*Cyanerpes lucidus*	Shining Honeycreeper	Mielero Luciente (Picudo Patiamarillo)	R			
807	*Cyanerpes cyaneus*	Red-legged Honeycreeper	Mielero Patirrojo (Picudo, Mielero, Tucuso, Trepador)	R			
808	*Dacnis venusta*	Scarlet-thighed Dacnis	Mielero Celeste y Negro (Calzones Rojos)	R			
809	*Dacnis cayana*	Blue Dacnis	Mielero Azulejo (Rey de Viuda)	R			
810	*Coereba flaveola*	Bananaquit	Reinita Mielera (Pincha Flor, Santa Marta)	R			
811	*Tiaris olivaceus*	Yellow-faced Grassquit	Semillerito Cariamarillo (Gallito)	R			
812	*Pinaroloxias inornata*	Cocos Finch	Pinzón de la Isla del Coco	R-END			
813	*Sporophila lineola*	Lined Seedeater	Espiguero Bigotudo (Setillero)	A			
814	*Sporophila funerea*	Thick-billed Seed-Finch	Semillero Picogrueso	R			
815	*Sporophila nuttingi*	Nicaraguan Seed-Finch	Semillero Piquirrosado	R-END			
816	*Sporophila corvinaC*	Variable Seedeater	Espiguero Variable (Setillero Collarejo, Monjito, Arrocerito)	R			
817	*Sporophila schistaceaO*	Slate-colored Seedeater	Espiguero Pizarroso (Setillero)	R			
818	*Sporophila torqueolaR*	White-collared Seedeater	Espiguero Collarejo (Setillero Collarejo)	R			
819	*Sporophila nigricollis*	Yellow-bellied Seedeater	Espiguero Vientriamarillo (Setillero Panameño)	R			
820	*Sporophila minuta*	Ruddy-breasted Seedeater	Espiguero Menudo (Setillero Ladrillo)	R			
821	*Emberizoides herbicola*	Wedge-tailed Grass-Finch	Sabanero Coludo (Chicharrón)	R			
822	*Saltator atriceps*	Black-headed Saltator	Saltator Cabecinegro (Chayotero)	R			
823	*Saltator maximus*	Buff-throated Saltator	Saltator Gorgianteado (Chayotero, Chojui, Comepuntas, Sinsonte Verde)	R			
824	*Saltator grossus*	Slate-colored Grosbeak	Picogrueso Piquirrojo	R			
825	*Saltator coerulescens*	Grayish Saltator	Saltator Grisáceo (Comepuntas, Come Chayote, Sensontle, Sinsonte)	R			
826	*Saltator striatipectus*	Streaked Saltator	Saltator Listado	R			

	Genus Incertae Sedis						
827	*Rhodinocichla rosea*	Rosy Thrush-Tanager	Tangara Pechirrosada (Queo)	R			
828	*Mitrospingus cassinii*	Dusky-faced Tanager	Tangara Carinegruzca	R			
	Emberizidae (25)						
829	*Pselliophorus tibialis*	Yellow-thighed Finch	Saltón de Muslos Amarillos (Calzones Amarillos)	R-END			
830	*Pezopetes capitalis*	Large-footed Finch	Saltón Patigrande	R-END			
831	*Arremon aurantiirostris*	Orange-billed Sparrow	Pinzón Piquinaranja (Pico Chile, Pico Rojo, Pico de Oro)	R			
832	*Arremon crassirostris*	Sooty-faced Finch	Pinzón Barranquero	R-END			
833	*Arremon brunneinucha*	Chestnut-capped Brush-Finch	Saltón Cabecicastaño	R			
834	*Arremon costaricensis*	Costa Rican Brush-Finch	Saltón Cabecinegro, Saltón Costarricense AOCR	R-END			
835	*Arremonops rufivirgatus*	Olive Sparrow	Pinzón Aceitunado (Timbón)	R			
836	*Arremonops conirostris*	Black-striped Sparrow	Pinzón Cabecilistado (Purisquero, Pájaro Suzuki)	R			
837	*Atlapetes albinucha*	White-naped Brush-Finch	Saltón Gargantiamarilla (Comepuntas, Purisco)	R			
838	*Aimophila rufescens*	Rusty Sparrow	Sabanero Rojizo	R			
839	*Melozone leucotis*	White-eared Ground-Sparrow	Pinzón Orejiblanco (Cuatro Ojos, Payasito)	R			
840	*Melozone biarcuata*	Prevost's Ground-Sparrow	Pinzón Cafetalero (Jupa Roja, Rey de Comemaíz, Mercenario)	R			
841	*Peucaea ruficauda*	Stripe-headed Sparrow	Sabanero Cabecilistado (Pájaro Chicle, Albarda Nueva, Ratoncillo)	R			
842	*Peucaea botterii*	Botteri's Sparrow	Sabanero Pechianteado	R			
843	*Spizella passerina*	Chipping Sparrow	Chimbito Común	A			
844	*Spizella pallida*	Clay-colored Sparrow	Chimbito o Chingolo Pálido	A			
845	*Chondestes grammacus*	Lark Sparrow	Sabanero Arlequín	M			
846	*Passerculus sandwichensis*	Savannah Sparrow	Sabanero Zanjero	A			
847	*Ammodramus savannarum*	Grasshopper Sparrow	Sabanero Colicorto	R, M			
848	*Melospiza lincolnii*	Lincoln's Sparrow	Sabanero de Lincoln	M			

849	*Zonotrichia capensis*	Rufous-collared Sparrow	Chingolo (Comemaíz, Pirrís)	R				
850	*Junco vulcani*	Volcano Junco	Junco Paramero (Junco Volcanero)	R-END				
851	*Chlorospingus flavopectus*	Common Chlorospingus	Tangara de Monte Ojeruda (Cuatro Ojos)	R				
852	*Chlorospingus pileatus*	Sooty-capped Chlorospingus	Tangara de Monte Cejiblanca	R-END				
853	*Chlorospingus canigularis*	Ashy-throated Chlorospingus	Tangara de Monte Gargantigrís	R				
	Cardinalidae (20)							
854	*Piranga flava*	Hepatic Tanager	Tangara Bermeja (Cardenal)	R				
855	*Piranga rubra*	Summer Tanager	Tangara Veranera (Cardenal Veranero, Pan de Achiote, Sangre Toro)	M				
856	*Piranga olivacea*	Scarlet Tanager	Tangara Escarlata (Cardenal Alas Negras)	M				
857	*Piranga ludoviciana*	Western Tanager	Tangara Carirroja	M				
858	*Piranga bidentata*	Flame-colored Tanager	Tangara Dorsirrayada (Cardenal)	R				
859	*Piranga leucoptera*	White-winged Tanager	Tangara Aliblanca (Cardenalito)	R				
860	*Habia rubica*	Red-crowned Ant-Tanager	Tangara Hormiguera Coronirroja (Relicario)	R				
861	*Habia fuscicauda*	Red-throated Ant-Tanager	Tangara Hormiguera Gorgirroja	R				
862	*Habia atrimaxillaris*	Black-cheeked Ant-Tanager	Tangara Hormiguera Carinegra	R-END				
863	*Chlorothraupis carmioli*	Carmiol's Tanager	Tangara Aceitunada o de Carmiol	R				
864	*Caryothraustes poliogaster*	Black-faced Grosbeak	Picogrueso Carinegro (Sarapiqueña)	R				
865	*Pheucticus tibialis*	Black-thighed Grosbeak	Picogrueso Vientriamarillo (Chorcho, Maizero, Chiltote)	R-END				
866	*Pheucticus ludovicianus*	Rose-breasted Grosbeak	Picogrueso Pechirrosado (Calandria)	M				
867	*Pheucticus melanocephalus*	Black-headed Grosbeak	Picogrueso Cabecinegro	A- SC				
868	*Amaurospiza concolor*	Blue Seedeater	Semillero Azulado	R				

869	*Cyanocompsa cyanoides*	Blue-black Grosbeak	Picogrueso Negro Azulado	R			
870	*Passerina caerulea*	Blue Grosbeak	Picogrueso Azul (Alondra)	R, M			
871	*Passerina cyanea*	Indigo Bunting	Azulillo Norteño (Indris)	M			
872	*Passerina ciris*	Painted Bunting	Azulillo Sietecolores (Arcoiris, Siete Colores)	M			
873	*Spiza americana*	Dickcissel	Sabanero Arrocero (Arrocero, Pius)	M			
	Icteridae (24)						
874	*Dolichonyx oryzivorus*	Bobolink	Tordo Arrocero	M			
875	*Agelaius phoeniceus*	Red-winged Blackbird	Tordo Sargento (Sargento)	R			
876	*Sturnella militaris*	Red-breasted Blackbird	Tordo Pechirrojo	R			
877	*Sturnella magna*	Eastern Meadowlark	Zacatero Común (Zacatera, Carmelo)	R			
878	*Xanthocephalus xanthocephalus*	Yellow-headed Blackbird	Tordo Cabecidorado	A			
879	*Dives dives*	Melodious Blackbird	Tordo Cantor	R			
880	*Quiscalus mexicanus*	Great-tailed Grackle	Clarinero, Zanate Grande (Sanate, Zanate)	R			
881	*Quiscalus nicaraguensis*	Nicaraguan Grackle	Clarinero, Zanate de Laguna (Totí, Garrapatero)	R-END			
882	*Molothrus bonariensis*	Shiny Cowbird	Vaquero Mirlo	R			
883	*Molothrus aeneus*	Bronzed Cowbird	Vaquero Ojirrojo (Pius)	R			
884	*Molothrus oryzivorus*	Giant Cowbird	Vaquero Grande	R			
885	*Icterus prosthemelas*	Black-cowled Oriole	Bolsero Capuchinegro (Chorcha del Platanar, Cacique Amarillo)	R			
886	*Icterus spurius*	Orchard Oriole	Bolsero Castaño (Cacique Ahumado)	M			
887	*Icterus chrysater*	Yellow-backed Oriole	Bolsero Dorsidorado	A			
888	*Icterus mesomelas*	Yellow-tailed Oriole	Bolsero Coliamarillo (Chorcha, Chiltote, Chiltotel)	R			
889	*Icterus pustulatus*	Streak-backed Oriole	Bolsero Dorsilistado (Chilchote, Chilto, Chorchín, Chorcha)	R			
890	*Icterus bullockii*	Bullock's Oriole	Bolsero de Bullock	A			

891	*Icterus pectoralis*	Spot-breasted Oriole	Bolsero Pechimanchado (Balsero, Chiltote)	R				
892	*Icterus galbula*	Baltimore Oriole	Bolsero Norteño (Cacique Veranero, Cacicón, Naranjero)	M				
893	*Amblycercus holosericeus*	Yellow-billed Cacique	Cacique Picoplata (Pico de Plata)	R				
894	*Cacicus uropygialis*	Scarlet-rumped Cacique	Cacique Lomiescarlata (Sargento, Plío)	R				
895	*Psarocolius decumanus*	Crested Oropendola	Oropéndola Crestada	R				
896	*Psarocolius wagleri*	Chestnut-headed Oropendola	Oropéndola Cabecicastaña (Oropéndola, Oropel, Guacalillo)	R				
897	*Psarocolius montezuma*	Montezuma Oropendola	Oropéndola de Moctezuma (Oropéndola)	R				
	Fringillidae (12)							
898	*Euphonia affinis*	Scrub Euphonia	Eufonia Gargantinegra (Finito, Agüío, Monjita Fina)	R				
899	*Euphonia luteicapilla*	Yellow-crowned Euphonia	Eufonia Coroniamarilla (Monjita, Agüío)	R-END				
900	*Euphonia laniirostris*	Thick-billed Euphonia	Eufonia Piquigruesa (Agüío)	R				
901	*Euphonia hirundinacea*	Yellow-throated Euphonia	Eufonia Gorgiamarilla (Agüío, Caciquita)	R				
902	*Euphonia elegantissima*	Elegant Euphonia	Eufonia Capuchiceleste (Agüío, Monjita, Caciquita)	R				
903	*Euphonia imitans*	Spot-crowned Euphonia	Eufonia Vientrirrojiza (Agüío Barranquillo)	R-END				
904	*Euphonia gouldi*	Olive-backed Euphonia	Eufonia Olivácea (Agüío, Barranquillo, Culo Rojo, Güere)	R				
905	*Euphonia minuta*	White-vented Euphonia	Eufonia Menuda (Finito Canario, Canarito, Canaria, Agüio)	R				
906	*Euphonia anneae*	Tawny-capped Euphonia	Eufonia Gorricanela (Agüío, Barranquilla)	R-END				
907	*Chlorophonia callophrys*	Golden-browed Chlorophonia	Clorofonia Cejidorada (Rualdo, Rey de Rualdo)	R-END				
908	*Spinus xanthogastrus*	Yellow-bellied Siskin	Jilguero Vientriamarillo (Mozotillo de Montaña)	R				
909	*Spinus psaltria*	Lesser Goldfinch	Jilguero Menor (Mozotillo de Charral)	R				

	Passeridae (1)						
910	*Passer domesticus*	House Sparrow	Gorrión Común (Electricista)	R			
	Estrildidae (1)						
911	*Lonchura malacca*	Tricolored Munia	Monjita Tricolor	R			

La AOCR es una organización abierta a todo público. El perfil del asociado/a es muy simple: ser amante de la naturaleza y tener deseos de aprender sobre las aves.

Cuota anual (enero - diciembre)
Socio regular: 10.000 colones
Socio estudiante: 5.000 colones

Puede cancelar personalmente en una charla de la AOCR o puede depositar la cuota en la cuenta de la Asociación en el Banco Nacional de Costa Rica, según la información en el cuadro. Después, envía una notificación a walcoca46@gmail.com. Debe incluir el número del depósito, además de los datos personales: nombre, apellidos, dirección electrónica y postal, teléfono y número de cédula.

Asociación Ornitológica de Costa Rica
Apartado 2289-1002, San José, Costa Rica

http://avesdecostarica.org

La Asociación Ornitológica de Costa Rica (AOCR) fue fundada en 1993 para investigar, divulgar y promover diversas actividades que difundan el conocimiento de la avifauna costarricense y contribuyen a la conservación de las poblaciones silvestres y sus respectivos habitats.

Tipo de cuenta	Moneda	Oficina	Cuenta	Dígito
Corriente	Colones	061	000492	5
Cliente 15106110010004923 Cédula: 3-002-145040				

La AOCR ofrece una charla y una gira el domingo mensual. Consulte a http://avesdecostarica.org para más información.

Los artículos de *Zeledonia* están indexados por LATINDEX (www.latindex.unam.mx) y OWL (Ornithological Worldwide Literature) birdlit.org, Dialnet y EBSCO. Zeledonia se ha incorporado en la Biblioteca Digital del Caribe de la Universidad de Florida: www.dloc.com.

El *Boletín Zeledonia* se publica semestralmente: junio y noviembre. Se distribuye electrónicamente a la membresía de la AOCR y por solicitud a bibliotecas y oganizaciones afines.

Junta Directiva

Asociación Ornitológica de Costa Rica
Apartado 2269-1002, San José, Costa Rica

Printed in Great Britain
by Amazon

15571927R00031